PRAISE FOR *THE DOUBLE WIN*...

Rodney's book is a proven roadmap to health in your work, your faith, and your family. Every chapter is simultaneously entertaining, inspiring, and incredibly practical for real-life issues. This message is so needed in our culture. I needed it! I'm thankful for *The Double Win*, and you'll be thankful for this book too.

—Dave Willis, Pastor, Podcaster, and Author

The Double Win is a timely and thought-provoking book to help you avoid the almost inevitable collision between your "calling" to your career and your family. I lived it. Rodney Gage gives busy individuals and families the godly, practical wisdom, and logical steps to say no to the many good options so they can say yes to the best.

—Dave Brat, PhD, Dean, School of Business, Liberty University

My friend Rodney Gage had me at "Work and at Home" in the subtitle of his latest book *The Double Win*. Relationally healthy people don't live compartmentalized lives. We all live by patterns. You can't be one way at home and another at work. There are names, even memes, for those who do! No doubt, living a congruous life is healthy, winning, and helpful to you and those around you. Go for *The Double Win*.

—Sam Chand, Leadership Consultant and author of *Change Has Changed* (www.samchand.com)

I have watched up close as Rodney has lived out the message of this book. He has the moral authority and the gifting to help you accomplish the double win!

—Shawn Lovejoy, Founder & CEO, CourageToLead

Finally, a book that provides actual steps to help create balance and success in your personal and professional life. As a wife, mother, and executive leader, the demands are high, and the North Star can become dim. Not only can I apply these principles in my own life, but I can help those around me to create a broader impact.

—Emily Gray, SVP, Customer Success and SaaS Executive

Rodney Gage's book challenges readers to focus on what truly matters and reevaluate what is necessary versus what is negotiable. The Double Win is an incredible resource that gives practical ways to incorporate work with God's purpose for your life. An excellent read!

—Penny Nance, CEO and President, Concerned Women for America

THE DOUBLE WIN

8 QUESTIONS EVERYONE MUST ASK
TO WIN AT WORK AND AT HOME

RODNEY GAGE

INSPIRE

Published by Inspire

Cover design by: Eric Powell
Cover Photo by: Andrew van Tilborgh

ISBN: 978-1-957369-08-2 1 2 3 4 5 6 7 8 9 10

Printed in the United States of America

DEDICATION

I want to dedicate this book to my wife, Michelle, our three children, Rebecca, Ashlyn, Luke, and our two fabulous sons-in-law, Daniel and Dillon. My greatest joy in life is doing life with them. My greatest reward is watching them live out the principles outlined in this book in their own lives and families. I couldn't be more proud of who they have become.

CONTENTS

Acknowledgments ix

Introduction: A No-Win Situation? 11

PART 1. RETHINK 23

1. The Motives Question: What's Driving Your Decisions? 25

2. The Beliefs Question: Who or What Makes You Happy? 47

3. The Dream Question: What Does Your Future Look Like?. 67

PART 2. REFOCUS 83

4. The Values Question: What Do You Want to Be Known For? . .85

5. The Priorities Question: What's (Really) Important to You? . . .105

6. The Expectations Question: Who Does What by When? 125

PART 3. REENGAGE 143

7. The Success Question: How Do You Define the Win? 145

8. The Legacy Question: How Will You Influence the Next Generation? 163

About the Author. 179

ACKNOWLEDGMENTS

I am a firm believer that we is greater than me. I can't imagine attempting a project like writing a book alone. It takes a team of people to bring ideas, research, stories, creativity, and life experiences to help a book project become a reality. I want to thank my wife, Michelle, whom I love, cherish, and respect so much. Her wisdom, encouragement, discernment, and input are always spot-on. I would also like to thank Pat Springle for his writing skills and wisdom. We have worked together for over thirty years. Lastly, I would like to thank the Dream Team of staff and people of ReThink Life Church. We have a saying as a church: "Let's do great things together." Together, we are helping families build strong relationships, so they can achieve the Double Win.

INTRODUCTION

A NO-WIN SITUATION?

You can't expect people to do well in their business if they've got problems at home.
—S. TRUETT CATHY, FOUNDER OF CHICK-FIL-A

In 2000, my wife, Michelle, who was eight months pregnant, and I, along with our two daughters (two and four years old), left our family, friends, familiar surroundings, and a brand new home we had recently built to move to Orlando, Florida, to pursue a dream to start a church. It was the most significant step of faith we had ever taken. Before we made this radical decision, we sought counsel from several friends who had started churches. We also met with consultants to determine if we were good candidates for the daunting challenge. Everyone warned us that it would be much more difficult than we imagined. They reminded us that

32 percent of church plants fail within four years.[1] I was determined to be in the percentage that made it!

When we moved to Orlando, we didn't know anyone. Even though we had a sponsoring church, we had no experience in starting a church from scratch, no building, and of course, no staff. Like any entrepreneur launching a business, I found myself wearing every hat.

We put in long hours sitting in endless organizational meetings, setting up the legal status and bank accounts, branding, marketing, planning events, raising funds, recruiting volunteers, purchasing equipment, finding rental space, and preparing for the launch. It was overwhelming! Did I mention that Michelle was eight months pregnant? Very soon, we were operating on fumes with little sleep.

We lived in a small rented home with no bathtub and a shower that could do little more than drip. The house had a faulty electrical breaker. Whenever Michelle wanted to use a hairdryer, we had to unscrew the light bulbs over the mirror to avoid blowing the breaker. (We learned that trick slowly, but we finally got it.) We had an invasion of fleas, which we later discovered came from dead raccoons under our house, and we had an attack of ants that crawled everywhere. We stored our furniture and the boxes of household things in the garage which flooded in a massive storm.

In the middle of all this, one day I stared into heaven and asked God, "What in the ________ are You doing? Why are we experiencing all of this? God, we're doing this for You! Why is this so hard?"

Fast-forward a few months. Michelle had given birth to our third child, and now we gave birth to our first worship service—it was Easter Sunday, 2001. What an exciting day! The dream in our hearts had finally become a reality, but the real work had just begun. Our responsibilities

1 Edward Stetzer and Warren Bird, "The State of Church Planting in the United States," 7.

increased, and the pressures and demands intensified. People wanted to meet for counseling, and volunteers needed training. Since they were volunteers, they were available to meet only early in the morning or in the evening. I found myself working around the clock. I wished I could make the weeks longer so I had more time, but Sunday came every seven days. I spent Saturdays prepping for my messages, which left little time for our young family.

I'll never forget Michelle walking into my study one day after our first year in Orlando. She and the kids were getting ready to go to a park, and she asked if I was going to join them. She knew she didn't really need to ask because my answer was entirely predictable: "No, I'm too busy." She asked anyway, and when I told her I couldn't go, she looked at me and said, "Rodney, you have a choice. You can choose to be a father to your children, or you can choose to be the pastor of the church, but you can't do both unless something changes!" She let that sink in for a few seconds, and then she continued, "Your children need you. Your children want you. What good does it do to reach the whole city and lose your family in the process?"

At that moment, I came face to face with the stark reality that I was on an unsustainable trajectory, and something had to give. It wasn't that I didn't love them, and it wasn't that I didn't want to spend time with them. I felt angry and guilt gnawed at me, but I felt trapped because of the endless demands on my time, and frankly, I was utterly exhausted. I thought being a pastor would bring joy and fulfillment, but it had blown a huge hole in my spiritual, relational, and emotional tanks. I was running on empty. The brief exchange in the doorway that day with Michelle was the turning point. At that moment, I decided that I would put my family before the church. I determined that it would be more acceptable for the church to fall apart than my family. I've never regretted that decision.

Today, Michelle and I have three wonderful adult children who love God and are fulfilling their unique calling and purpose. Our two daughters are married to godly young men. We're so proud of who they have become and their impact on so many others.

Michelle and I have been married for over thirty years, and people often ask us, "What's your secret to a successful marriage and a close-knit family?" This book is the answer to that question. Even after weathering a global pandemic and countless difficulties associated with it, our church and our family are thriving. Like you, we're living in a world of pressure, compromise, unpredictability, constant distractions, and unrealistic demands between work and home. In this fast-paced, technology-driven world, everyone feels the stress, especially in our marriages and family relationships. Is it even possible to live a life that's healthy, functional, and fulfilling—at work and at home? The answer is "yes!" It's why I titled this book *The Double Win*. The concepts in these chapters will help you answer eight key questions, so you can get off the treadmill of stress and find balance, meaning, peace, and strength.

FIRST, THE GOOD NEWS

I have three primary goals for this book:

First, I want to comfort you. I know how you feel because I've felt this tension throughout my adult life, and I've learned some lessons (usually the hard way). In these pages, I hope you feel understood, and I hope you know that you're not alone in the struggle.

Second, I want to convince you that it's possible to win at home and at work. With God's help, we can restructure our priorities and find a new source of freedom and peace.

And third, I want to challenge you to rethink your priorities and your expectations in your marriage, with your kids, in your career, and how you spend your ever-shrinking free time.

The foundational principle I want to communicate is simple: You can't win at work if you're losing at home, and you can't win at home if you're losing at work. The two realms of life are inextricably connected. The questions and answers in the following chapters provide insights and practical steps for you.

The foundational principle I want to communicate is simple: You can't win at work if you're losing at home, and you can't win at home if you're losing at work. The two realms of life are inextricably connected.

AND NOW, THE BAD NEWS

All of us live with tension between work and home, but when the level of tension redlines, all kinds of negative things happen—to us, to our families, and to our productivity. According to the Mayo Clinic, unrelieved stress affects more than our moods; it has detrimental impacts on our bodies and our behavior, too. Physiologically, stress is said to settle on the weakest part of our bodies. Some of us have nagging headaches, others develop chronic gastrointestinal problems, and many suffer from muscle tightness, fatigue, and other forms of pain. Stress often causes our minds to race at night, so we have trouble sleeping. We're exhausted when we start each day, and it changes our desire (and our desirability) for sex.

Our moods may swing from depression to outbursts of anger; we feel overwhelmed by normal daily responsibilities and chronic anxiety. In attempts to numb the pain and grasp for the illusion of control, we may eat too much or too little, use substances to find some relief, use anger to intimidate, withdraw from people to avoid feeling vulnerable, escape online, or watch too much television.[2]

These effects don't just go away on their own. Dr. Kerry Ressler, professor of psychiatry at Harvard Medical School, reports on brain research that found significant changes in our brains when we experience too much stress for too long. Stress triggers "survival wiring" which focuses the brain's resources on fighting, fleeing, or freezing . . . and away from calm logic and reasoning. The Harvard Health article states:

> *Researchers believe that when one part of your brain is engaged, the other parts of your brain may not have as much energy to handle their own vital tasks, he says. For example, if you are in a dangerous or emotionally taxing situation, the amygdala (the part of your brain that governs your survival instincts) may take over, leaving the parts of your brain that help to store memories and perform higher-order tasks with less energy and ability to get their own jobs done. "The basic idea is that the brain is shunting its resources because it's in survival mode, not memory mode," says Dr. Ressler. This is why you might be more*

2 "How Stress Affects Your Body and Behavior," Mayo Foundation for Medical Education and Research, *Mayo Clinic*, 24 Mar. 2021, https://www.mayoclinic.org/healthy-lifestyle/stress-management/in-depth/stress-symptoms/art-20050987.

forgetful when you are under stress or may even experience memory lapses during traumatic events.[3]

So, when someone says, "It's all in your head," that's right, but not in the way they mean it!

Of course, the initial source of increased levels of stress may be work or home (or for that matter, health problems, financial issues, etc.), but soon, it affects every aspect of our lives. In other words, we always "take our work home with us," even if we don't talk about it specifically and in detail. The pressure of expectations hangs like a dark cloud over us, and we rain on everyone close by. Little annoyances result in big explosions, and everyone finds a role to play to lower the temperature: some try to "read the room" and jump in to fix others' problems, some use humor to distract from the anger and hurt, some use their explosive anger like erupting volcanoes to dominate and control, and some hide (behind a book, in their rooms, or by the screens on their phones) to avoid being the target of outbursts and glares of contempt.

Our lives have become much more complicated and fast-paced than only a few decades ago. Our kids are involved in more activities, so we have to coordinate their schedules as best we can. We spend more time in the car, more time at work (even if we're working from home), and more time trying to recoup from all the demands. Our devices are always on, so our attention is always split between the person in front of us, the task we're trying to accomplish, and our readiness to answer every text and tweet. (Email is so yesterday!) When we "rest," it's more like crashing emotionally and physically than genuine, restorative relaxation. And then we're off to the next thing.

---

3 "Protect Your Brain from Stress," *Harvard Health Publishing,* 15 Feb. 2021, https://www.health.harvard.edu/mind-and-mood/protect-your-brain-from-stress.

Psychologists and family counselors identify four main causes of disagreement between spouses: money, children, sex, and in-laws. Even the healthiest marriages have to navigate these rough waters, but when high levels of stress are factored in, these topics can lead to declarations of war! Each person has to win instead of trying to find common ground, they make excuses instead of taking responsibility, the children live with pervasive confusion about how to cope with the hurt, fear, anger, and shame, and the best they can all hope for is a negotiated cease-fire. For many couples, the unthinkable solution of divorce becomes an increasingly attractive option.

I've heard people say, "When I'm at home, I can't stop thinking about all I need to do at work, and when I'm at work, I worry about my relationships with my spouse and kids." Being distracted at work can harm a career, and it can cost companies a lot of money. According to the Corporate Research Project performed by Life Innovations and The Marriage CoMission, businesses in America lose $6 billion annually due to decreased productivity stemming from marriage and family difficulties. Marriage and family issues not only cause absenteeism but presenteeism (being physically present but mentally and emotionally absent). This results in low performance, lack of focus, poor judgement, and bad decision making, along with low morale and motivation.[4]

A compilation of research on the impact of employee stress reports:

» 83 percent of US workers suffer from work-related stress.
» US businesses lose up to $300 billion yearly as a result of workplace stress.
» Stress causes around one million workers to miss work every day.

4 Turvey, Matthew D, and David H Olson, *Marriage and Family Wellness Corporate America's Business?* Life Innovations, Inc., 2006, https://rw360.org/wp-content/uploads/2017/04/Marriage-and-Family-Wellness-Corporate-America-1.pdf.

- Only 43 percent of US employees think their employers care about their work-life balance.
- Depression leads to $51 billion in costs due to absenteeism and $26 billion in treatment costs.
- Work-related stress causes 120,000 deaths and results in $190 billion in healthcare costs yearly.
- Those between 30 and 49 years old suffer the most stress.
- 52 percent of Generation Z (born between 1997 and 2012) have been diagnosed with mental health problems.[5]

Do you see yourself in any of the descriptions and statistics about the vortex of stress at home and at work? I hope not, but virtually everyone experiences heightened levels of stress these days. In fact, it's become the water we swim in, so we don't even notice it any longer.

REAL PEOPLE, REAL CHANGE

The principles in this book are transferable for everyone; however, couples, parents, and blended families are struggling most when it comes to juggling the demands between work and home. I realize that the dynamics of parenting have shifted with so many single parents and blended families in our country today. According to *The Daily Wire*, only 18 percent of American households are married couples and their families.[6]

Regardless of your current situation—married, single parent, blended family, grandparents, or anyone thinking of getting married and having children one day—you will benefit greatly by thinking through the

5 "42 Worrying Workplace Stress Statistics," *Stress.org*, 25 Sep. 2019, https://www.stress.org/42-worrying-workplace-stress-statistics.

6 Ben Zeisloft, "Only 18% of American Households are Families with Married Parents," *The Daily Wire*, 8 Dec. 2021, https://www.dailywire.com/news/only-18-of-american-households-are-families-with-married-parents.

eight questions and answers in this book. You may look at your current stress level and wonder if there's any hope at all. I assure you, there is, but the process of change won't be easy. As we begin, let me make a few recommendations:

- There are plenty of changes we can make in our schedules and priorities so our lives become at least a little more sane, but under all of those is a spiritual issue: What gives us meaning and purpose? And what are our lives about anyway? We'll undoubtedly find that it's very hard to say "no" to things that have felt utterly indispensable and normal, so we need a new frame of reference. We need to look to God—not our careers, our titles, our good looks, our income, or our popularity—as our North Star.
- As a person of faith, I can testify firsthand, unless we put God in the center of our lives, we're destined to stay on the treadmill of trying hard but always needing to do more. But in Him, we can experience peace, find wisdom to make better choices, and truly enjoy the people He has put in our lives. Jesus is inviting us to join Him in this journey:

  "Are you weary, carrying a heavy burden? Come to me. I will refresh your life, for I am your oasis. Simply join your life with mine. Learn my ways and you'll discover that I'm gentle, humble, easy to please. You will find refreshment and rest in me. For all that I require of you will be pleasant and easy to bear." —Matthew 11:28-30
- Do you believe this promise? Are you willing to accept His invitation?
- Be honest with at least one person. One of our biggest problems is that we assume we're the only ones who are struggling. I assure you that's not true—I'm one of them myself! We need someone who

will listen without judging and love without smothering us with suggestions.

» Involve people in the solution. Talk to your spouse, your older kids, a pastor, a friend, and maybe some trusted people at work about your path of reconstructing your life to manage stress and live more authentically—but be selective. Not everyone will understand, and not everyone will be supportive, but some will.

» Be equally hopeful and tenacious. Brain wiring doesn't change easily. It takes concerted effort over time to cut new grooves of neural pathways, but it's certainly possible. There will be times when you want to quit, times when it seems too hard, times when you don't see much progress. Stick with it. God's love and strength are available to you 24/7. Your fulfillment, happiness, and the love of your family and friends are worth it all.

At the end of this introduction and each of the chapters, you'll find a few questions to stimulate your thinking and guide your application. You can also use these questions for discussions with your spouse, your children, and some good friends.

THINK ABOUT IT:

In your own life, or in the life of someone you know, how have you seen stress at work affect family life and stress in the family affect the person's productivity and relationships at work?

Which of the statistics and descriptions of stress stand out to you? Why are these significant?

What do you hope to get out of this book?

PART 1

RETHINK

CHAPTER 1

THE MOTIVES QUESTION: WHAT'S DRIVING YOUR DECISIONS?

People don't buy into what you do; they buy why you do it.
And what you do simply proves what you believe.
—Simon Sinek

When you fly on Delta Airlines from anywhere in the Southern part of the country, you'll probably connect through Atlanta. Hartsfield-Jackson Atlanta International Airport may have the longest name in the world, and it has more passengers than any other airport in the world—about 43 million a year. The concourses are connected by trams, or you can walk between them if you have enough time (I don't recommend it). I seldom have enough time. Not long ago, my flight arrived on A Concourse, and wouldn't you know it, my next flight was on the opposite side of the airport out of the E Concourse. Our incoming flight was late, so I ran to the tram, tried to will it to move faster, and then ran as fast as I could huffing and puffing to the gate. The gate attendant grimaced and said, "I'm sorry, but we've already shut the doors. You can check with the desk for the next flight."

That incident taught me (again) that I need to be sure I have plenty of time to breathe between flights, especially when I'm flying through Atlanta . . . and especially on Friday afternoons and evenings when everyone and their cousin in Georgia and the surrounding states is in line to fly home.

Margin. It's a simple word that's packed with practical applications. It's the space between events that gives us time to breathe, think, and rest, if only for a few moments.

Margin. It's a simple word that's packed with practical applications. It's the space between events that gives us time to breathe, think, and rest, if only for a few moments. In his brilliant book on this topic, physician Richard Swenson observes:

> *We must have some room to breathe. We need freedom to think and permission to heal. Our relationships are being starved to death by velocity. No one has the time to listen, let alone love. Our children lay wounded on the ground, run over by our high-speed good intentions. Is*

God now pro-exhaustion? Doesn't He lead people beside the still waters anymore? Who plundered those wide-open spaces of the past, and how can we get them back? There are no fallow lands for our emotions to lie down and rest in.[7]

The factor that drives our decisions is found in one word: more. If we can only get one more thing accomplished, we believe, we'll feel better about ourselves, and just as important, we'll impress anyone who's watching. The push to have more stuff, make more money, be more successful, and be more impressive erodes (or clobbers) any sense of margin. We equate speed with success and busyness with productivity. We're often late, overworked, overcommitted, and exhausted, and we wonder why life is so hard.

In his article, "Diagnosing Hurry Sickness" in *Leadership* magazine, pastor and author John Ortberg identified two common signs of stress: speeding up and multitasking.

1) "Speeding up. You are haunted by the fear that you don't have enough time to do what needs to be done. You try to read faster, lead board meetings more efficiently, write [business plans or emails] on the fly. . . ."
2) "Multiple-tasking. You find yourself doing or thinking more than one thing at a time. The car is a favorite place for this. Hurry-sick people may drive, eat, drink coffee, listen to podcasts for ideas, shave or apply make-up, direct business on the car phone—all at the same time. Or they may try to watch TV, read email, eat dinner, and carry on a phone conversation simultaneously."[8]

Why in the world do we live like this? Because we've convinced ourselves of three things that aren't really true.

---

7 Richard Swenson, MD, *Margin* (Colorado Springs: NavPress, 2004), 30.
8 John Ortberg, "Diagnosing Hurry Sickness," *Leadership*, Fall, 1998.

THREE LIES

I know these three statements are really common because I hear them (and say them and think them) so often.

#1 "There's not enough time to do everything I have to do!"

Maybe the problem isn't the lack of time but too many things on the to-do list. We say "yes" to too many things, and when we think of saying "no," we feel guilty or deficient—or more likely, that we're falling behind our friends who live at an even more frantic pace than we do. We press, we speed, we strain to get one more thing done, and we're quick to add "just one more."

When we insist there's not enough time to get things done, we need to remember that our gracious God has given us all the time we need to do what He wants us to do. To find margin, we need to learn to say "no" more often.

#2 "I'm just in a busy season right now. It'll be different soon."

Maybe, maybe not. The problem is that we're so driven to pack more things into our schedules that any margin is quickly eaten up by our next overcommitment. We're creatures of habit—good habits and bad ones. When we've been pushing for more than a couple of weeks, we've created a habit that's hard to break. Things won't "go back to the way they used to be" without changing the trajectory of our thoughts, choices, and behaviors. Busy people have only one season: it's called "busy!"

#3 "But this is really important!"

Yeah, I know. I've said this far too many times. It's the default excuse to avoid making hard decisions to say "no" to anything. Too often, we confuse the urgent for the important, and we live for the adrenaline rush we get when we kick into high gear. In this way, everything is "really important" because every task and every appointment is a chance to prove that we're competent and worthy of acclaim. But this excuse isn't limited to our internal conversation; we hear this message from our boss, our partners, our spouse, our kids, our parents, and everyone else who has a claim on our time and energy.

Let me show how this works from a popular story from the Bible. The Gospel writer Luke takes us to the scene:

> *As Jesus and the disciples continued on their journey, they came to a village where a woman welcomed Jesus into her home. Her name was Martha and she had a sister named Mary. Mary sat down attentively before the Master, absorbing every revelation he shared. But Martha became exasperated with finishing the numerous household chores in preparation for her guests, so she interrupted Jesus and said, "Lord, don't you think it's unfair that my sister left me to do all the work by myself? You should tell her to get up and help me."*
>
> *The Lord answered her, "Martha, my beloved Martha. Why are you upset and troubled, pulled away by all these many distractions? Mary has discovered the one thing most important by choosing to sit at my feet. She is undistracted, and I won't take this privilege from her."* —Luke 10:38-42

Notice the progression:

» Martha started with good intentions: She "welcomed Jesus into her home."

» But she became focused on what was urgent: She "became exasperated with finishing the numerous household chores."

» When she was left alone to do the work, she was consumed with resentment and self-pity: "Lord, don't you think it's unfair?"
» And finally, she blamed her sister and demanded that Jesus obey her: "You should tell [Mary] to get up and help me."

What do we learn from watching this scene unfold? It's not that Martha was a bad person. She wanted to be a gracious host to her guests, but she was focused on the urgent instead of the important. When no one seemed to appreciate her efforts, she felt sorry for herself, and blamed her sister and Jesus for not caring enough. Sound familiar? That's what happens to us more times than we want to count. We begin with good intentions to help, care, and serve, but we don't have good margins in our lives, so we overcommit, which results in our feeling sorry for ourselves and blaming those who made the better decision to choose the important over the urgent.

CARVING OUT ENOUGH MARGIN

We can only enjoy the double win if we carve out some margin. To reorient our decision-making process, we need clear minds and courage to go against our entrenched habits. At first, new choices don't just feel awkward . . . they feel wrong! Fight through this resistance, talk to someone who will encourage you to keep moving in the right direction. It's important to develop a new set of beliefs about yourself, your responsibilities, and the way life should work. Here are the ones that I think are most important:

1. Accept your limitations.

News flash: you're human, and humans have limitations. We're not omniscient—knowing all things, and we're not omnipresent—able to be everywhere at once. We may try to act like Superman or Wonder

Woman, but that's our title or our job description. In fact, God has structured our lives with limitations to teach us humility and wisdom. We're humbled when we recognize our limitations, and we're wise when we choose what's important.

Unfortunately, we're not very adept at recognizing our limits. In fact, we constantly overestimate our abilities and underestimate the problems and how much time they will take. I do this all the time. When people ask me, "Can you do this today?" I often respond without thinking. I insist, "Sure, I'll add that in!" But I don't stop with one—I'll add eight or nine things. I plan on it taking five minutes, but instead, it takes half an hour. Instead of the meeting taking half an hour, it takes an hour. We're often blind to our limitations.

On top of that, we live in a culture that constantly tells us, "You can do it all! You can have it all! You can be it all! You can have everything! You can be whatever you want to be!" But that's a lie. You can go to all the self-help seminars in the world, but your future is limited by factors such as your intelligence and age. I may have a dream to play in the NBA, but my basketball abilities are somewhat hindered by the plain fact that I can't jump, I'm not fast, and I can't shoot. Other than that, send me a fat contract! No matter how much you want to, you're never going to be able to sing like Pavarotti or dance like Usher. You can take all the singing or dance classes in the world, but you're just not going to be that good. You don't have that natural ability. But here's the truth: You can be all that God wants you to be—and He is infinitely wise and loving.

We have physical limitations. You couldn't swim to Hawaii no matter how much positive thinking you did. You can't go six months without food no matter how much you try to talk yourself into it. There are limits to positive thinking. But people say, "What about that verse, 'I can do all things through Christ who strengthens me'?" Don't take that verse out of context. Can you fly? Of course you can't fly. That verse isn't saying that you can go beyond your human limits. Don't use that verse to conclude, "I can keep on taking more and more stress, more and more problems, more and more debt, more and more difficulties in my life. I can handle it all. I'll never collapse because 'I can do all things through Christ who strengthens me.'" That's nonsense and a misuse of the verse.

We also have emotional limitations. These are much harder for us to judge in our own lives. We know our physical limits. You know how far you can run before you collapse. You know how fast you can run a mile. But you don't know your own emotional limits. You can't carry ten people on your back out of a burning building, but some of us think we can carry ten people's emotional load of hurt, fear, bitterness, and shame. How many people's emotional needs can you carry? One? Five? Ten? What's your limit? At what point do you say, "Wait! That's more than I can handle"? Where do you draw the line?

We have mental limitations. Scientists are now discovering that the human mind can only handle so much new information at one time before it goes full tilt! But we live in a culture where the media is constantly pumping new information into our minds through news feeds, television, social media, and limitless websites. As a result, most Americans today are mentally fried. They can't handle any more. Scientists are studying the psychic damage of trying to cram so much in. How many technology manuals for gadgets in your house have you never read front to back? Why? You just can't handle it. I've got phones now that do fifty things. I just want it to answer when my wife calls me! I'm not going to read the manual or watch the YouTube tutorial because I can't handle the info overload.

And of course we have time limitations. No matter how many time management seminars you go to, you're never going to have more than twenty-four hours in a day. It's a limit . . . and you have to sleep part of that time. If anyone had a reason to be stressed out, it was Job. He suffered terrible calamities, but he recognized his limitations. He prayed, "Our time is limited. You, God, have given us only so many months to live and have set limits we cannot go beyond" (Job 14:5).

You're probably thinking, It would really be nice if God would warn me when I'm reaching my limit, if God would put a red flashing light in my brain or a beeper would go off, "Warning! Ninety-five percent! You're about to go on overload! Back off!" Wouldn't that be great if you had a warning light like that? Well, you do. It's called pain. It's called fatigue. It's called stress. It's called loss of joy. It's called irritability. When you're irritable, you're on overload. You've exceeded a limit—a physical, mental, spiritual, or emotional limit (or all of the above!). The starting point for building margin is to realize you have limits. If you just keep cramming your life full of more and more of everything, sooner or later you'll crash. Count on it. It's guaranteed.

2. Expect to have problems.

I'm all for planning. I'm all about preparing for contingencies. I'm all about having a detailed schedule, but I've had to admit that curveballs are a normal part of life. Former boxing champion Mike Tyson got it right when he said, "Everyone has a plan until they get punched in the mouth." If you think that you can have everything in your life go as planned, you ought to just go check into a mental health hospital right now. Virtually nothing goes as planned. I can't get an hour of my life to go as planned, much less a day, a week, a month, or my entire life. Plans are good. The

Bible says we ought to plan because good plans lead you in the right direction, but nothing ever goes perfectly. If your expectations are too high, you're setting yourself up for big disappointments.

This isn't an abstract philosophical concept. If I've got to drive somewhere, I know it's going to take me fifteen minutes if traffic is smooth. Can I count on that? It's a crap shoot—sometimes you win; sometimes you lose. How do you respond when you get caught in traffic? Are you calm and patient because you've built in plenty of margin, or are you growling at the slow driver in front of you and holding the steering wheel in a death grip? You know what can happen: There may be traffic. You may have a flat tire. You may get an urgent call and have to go somewhere else. You may forget something and have to go back. Some of us are late to work or church or our kids' practices half the time, and we blame everyone and anyone when we're delayed . . . everyone but ourselves. The fact that we're often late means there's not enough margin in our lives.

Jesus told us, "In the world you will have trouble" (John 16:33). He didn't say, "You might have trouble," or "You could have trouble." He said, "You're going to have trouble. Count on it." So why are we surprised? We assume that everything's going to go as planned. Actually, I'm preaching to myself. I am a naturally optimistic person, and I don't think about what could go wrong. I'm not wired that way. That's why I need people around me to say, "But what about this?" or "What about that?" I just don't think that way. I'm always saying, "It's all going to work out great. It's going to be fine. What problem?" I need to expect the unexpected. As the old saying goes: "Hope for the best but plan for the worst, and settle for anything in between." When we're wise enough to expect the unexpected, we follow King Solomon's advice: "The prudent person perceives difficulties ahead and takes precautions. The simpleton goes blindly on and suffers the consequences" (Proverbs 22:3).

3. Put space in your schedule.

In an article in the *Harvard Business Review* titled "4 Ways to Improve Your Strategic Thinking Skills," Nina Bowman cites her experience with an executive who asked to consult with her. Nina remembers:

> *In the early phase of our work together, Lisa kept a jam-packed schedule, running from meeting to meeting. She found it difficult to contribute strategically without the time to reflect on the issues and to ponder options. Recognizing that she was not bringing her full value to the table, she started to evaluate her tasks based on urgency and importance. . . . She stopped going to meetings she didn't need to be at. She blocked out thinking time on her calendar and honored it, just as she would for other meetings. And she fought back the initial guilt of "Am I doing real work when I'm just sitting at my desk thinking?"*[9]

Other people aren't going to put space in your schedule for thinking, relaxing, and recharging. If it's going to be there, you have to make it happen.

Other people aren't going to put space in your schedule for thinking, relaxing, and recharging. If it's going to be there, you have to make it

9 Nina A Bowman, "4 Ways to Improve Your Strategic Thinking Skills," *Harvard Business Review*, 7 Dec. 2016, https://hbr.org/2016/12/4-ways-to-improve-your-strategic-thinking-skills.

happen. Michael Hyatt says, "What gets scheduled get done."[10] The faster you go, the more margin you need. It's admirable to be known as a diligent worker and someone who's committed to the company, but when it makes us on edge all the time, and negatively affects our marriage and family, it's time to make some adjustments. It reminds me of the story of the guy who came home and his little kindergarten daughter asked him why he was working so hard and why he always had to bring work home. He looked at her and said, "I don't have time to get it all finished at work, so I need to bring it home and get it done." The daughter looked up at him and said, "Daddy, I think they should put you in the slower group."

We don't get bonus points for working ourselves to death. It's not admirable to be a hero at work and a zero at home. It's not commendable to fill up every waking moment. Some of us are so busy because we don't want to think and feel—it's too painful. But others want the high we get from always being in a hurry. There's a better way to live. Carve out empty space and enjoy it.

4. Be a great gardener, and prune your schedule.

Pruning seems completely counterproductive. People who own vineyards absolutely butcher their vines down to the nubs each year. For those of us who don't know how it works, their labor looks like a huge mistake—but it's not at all. Pruning is the way they produce more grapes. It's the very best thing that can happen to the vines. Failure to prune actually stunts the growth of the vine and limits production.

Quite often, you can sprout new activity branches. You're doing some things now that you didn't do a year ago. You've added them to your

10 "Coalition Building: Staying focused on your priorities," Cited by *Jennifer Redmond Knight*, https://www.jredmondknight.com/2019/12/30/coalition-building-staying-focused-on-your-priorities/.

schedule. But here's the question: What have you cut out? What have you pruned back? You can't just keep adding and adding to your schedule. At every new season (start of a school year, a promotion, a move, starting a business, etc.), it's tempting to add more. Instead, it's smart to use these times to prune . . . sometimes radically.

Here's the secret: When gardeners prune, they don't just cut off deadwood. They cut off living branches that are very fruitful. In your pruning, you're going to have to cut out some activities that are still productive. You have to cut them off because you're in a new season that promises new, abundant growth, but only if you have the wisdom and courage to prune.

In his first letter to the Corinthians, the apostle Paul wrote, "It's true that our freedom allows us to do anything, but that doesn't mean that everything we do is good for us. I'm free to do as I choose, but I choose to never be enslaved to anything" (1 Corinthians 6:12). That means you and I are free to cram our lives full of activities—it's entirely our choice—but it's not good for us. And what about the part of being "enslaved"? Is that just hyperbole? No, when we're rushing around trying to do everything and we're frazzled and exhausted, we've become slaves to the unrealistic demands we've put on ourselves.

What's the solution? It's simple, profound, and difficult—learn to say "no." It's easy to say "no" to a root canal or an IRS audit, but it's far harder to say "no" to things you want to do (or that others want us to do). Our choices usually aren't between good things and bad things, but between good things and better things. A good thing can become a bad thing if it keeps you from the best thing. This means we have to prune a lot that we consider "good." We have to set priorities, to prune away a lot of good things (and all the bad, of course), so we can invest our energies and time in the better and best.

A good thing can become a bad thing if it keeps you from the best thing.

Selection is the key to an effective life. You'll be more effective if you figure out what you're not going to do as well as what you are going to do. The fact is that you'll actually accomplish more by doing less, by being totally committed to two or three things that really matter instead of being half-committed to a dozen different things.

How often do you need to prune? Gardeners prune after every productive season. They don't sit back and count on another bumper harvest. They do the hard and necessary work to cut back the productive vines so they'll be even more productive. I suggest we prune at least every quarter, at the start of every school year, every significant career transition, and whenever we find ourselves running around like a dog chasing its tail.

One more thing: If you don't want to prune the activities in your life, there's another method. God will do the pruning. He'll use failure, illness, financial setbacks, family disruption, wayward children, or some other crisis to get our attention. Choose Plan A. Plan B is much harder.

5. Bring God into the mix.

I've talked to a number of Christian marketplace leaders who have told me that they may have their devotions in the morning or listen to a podcast on their way to work, but they rarely bring God into the other parts of their day. They (and I'm looking in the mirror here) have compartmentalized God to the "spiritual parts" of their lives, and they've missed the opportunity to "practice the presence of God" all day every day. The result is that much of our lives are spent in self-dependence and self-effort, and we fail to tap into God's limitless resources of wisdom, love, and power.

My suspicion is that the more frantic our lives are, the less we trust God. As we prune our schedules, we have more space to think, pray, and relate to the people around us, and we trust God to do what only He can do. Don't get me wrong. I'm not suggesting that we become passive and hope God does everything. As followers of Jesus and ambassadors for Him, we're part of the family business to bring God's kingdom to earth as it is in heaven. That's quite a mission statement! We do that not only inside the walls of the church, but far more as we relate to our families, neighbors, colleagues, and friends. The apostle Paul wrote in his letter to the Philippians, "Now you must continue to make this new life fully manifested as you live in the holy awe of God—which brings you trembling into his presence. God will continually revitalize you, implanting within you the passion to do what pleases him" (Philippians 2:12-13). It's God's responsibility to lead and empower us; it's our responsibility to trust Him to fill us, direct us, and use us . . . and to obey in everything we do because He's imminently trustworthy.

As followers of Jesus and ambassadors for Him, we're part of the family business to bring God's kingdom to earth as it is in heaven.

KNOW YOUR WHY.

When we dig down below the surface of our emotions and lifestyle, we find the motive that drives all of our decisions: our most fundamental why. What really matters, above all else? Whom or what are we living for? Life is more—much more—than accolades, acquiring more stuff, or having a large platform or power over others. When these are most important, we pay a steep price in the relationships we value most: with God and the people we love. Are we paying attention to the signs of stress that misguided motivations and a lack of margin are having on our mood, our health, and our responses to people . . . or are we ignoring the signs and trying harder to do more to prove ourselves? God has given each of us the incredible invitation to trust Him and fulfill a higher purpose, to maximize our time, talents, and treasure to represent Jesus, being salt and light to those around us. We're made to make a difference.

There are many, many passages of scripture we can use as inspiring purpose statements. One of these is found in the apostle Paul's message in Antioch. He explains how the history of Israel points to the ultimate King, the Messiah, Jesus. In the middle of his history lesson, he explains that God replaced King Saul with a new king, David: "I have found David son of Jesse, a man after my own heart; he will do everything I want him to do" (Acts 13:22, NIV). Isn't that the purified essence of our God-given purpose: to know God and live for Him? But in countless conversations with people over the years, I've found that relatively few people have a clear, compelling sense of purpose. They may have a vague idea, or it may change from time to time, but it doesn't galvanize their hearts, minds, and choices, so they know they're making a difference. If we don't have a firm grip on our purpose, five unpleasant (and unnecessary) things will almost certainly happen:

1) Life seems useless.

King Solomon lamented, "Life is useless, all useless. You spend your life working, but what do you have to show for it?" (Ecclesiastes 1:2-4, TLB) That's the perception of a striking number of people, people we connect with every day. A *Forbes* article reported two different studies: one said that 40 percent of employees say their work is meaningless, and the other pegged that number at 24 percent.[11] There are, of course, many other places on the continuum from meaningless to meaningful. It's safe to say that a lot of people can't connect their life's purpose to their work.

2) Life is exhausting.

Again, we turn to King Solomon: "The sun rises and goes down. The wind blows round and round and back again. Every river flows into the sea then the water returns to where the river began and starts all over again. Everything leads to weariness" (Ecclesiastes 1:5-7, TLB). Do you ever feel like you live on a treadmill? You're using a lot of energy and engaged in a lot of activities, but there's no progress. The fact is, you can win the rat race, but you're still a rat! If you don't have a purpose in life, life seems useless and life seems tiresome.

3) Life is unfulfilling.

We get restless when we don't see the point in what we do each day. Once again, King Solomon explained, "No matter how much we see, we're never satisfied; no matter how much we hear, we're not content. History merely repeats itself" (Ecclesiastes 1:8, TLB).

11 Parna Mathur, "Do Meaningless Jobs Exist in America?" *Forbes*, 29 Nov. 2018, https://www.forbes.com/sites/aparnamathur/2018/11/29/do-meaningless-jobs-exist-in-america/?sh=34b735463269.

Instead of meaning, we look for distractions; instead of purpose, we find ways to escape the drudgery.

4) Life feels insignificant.

Emptiness. Boredom. Apathy. Hopelessness. I've heard people say that when they die, the impact they'll leave behind is the same as you get when you take your finger out of a glass of water. In other words, nothing! Again Solomon shared his wisdom: "No one remembers what has happened in the past, and no one in days to come will remember what happens between now and then" (Ecclesiastes 1:11, TLB).

When we don't have something to live for, our lives are filled with nothingness. We may have thought we were important before, but we've come to the conclusion that it's all been a waste. Have you ever been to a class reunion? It's humbling. People are getting fat and going bald—and those are the women! The guys . . . let's don't go there. If our hearts are set on wealth, status, titles, or power, we may feel like we have the world by the tail for a while, but only for a while. Sooner or later, we'll see the futility in those pursuits. You may already be there.

5) Life feels out of control.

Have you ever had vertigo? I have, and I still struggle with it from time to time. It's the worst feeling in the world. It comes upon you suddenly and violently. The room starts spinning, your stomach gets nauseous, and you feel completely out of control. Similarly, many of us suffer disorientation from "the appealing illusion of control," so we're vulnerable to almost any disturbance in our plans and expectations. We believe we can will things to be just like we want them: spouses, children, friends, work, body shape, finances, and everything else. When things don't go like we planned, we get bent out of shape. I can almost hear King Solomon laugh at the thought: "You can't straighten out what is crooked and you can't count things that aren't there!" (Ecclesiastes 1:15, TLB) We can't control the weather, we can't control events, and we can't control people. When things are broken, sometimes they're beyond repair no matter how hard we try to fix them.

When you remove God from the picture, the options for meaning and purpose are slim to none.

A life without purpose isn't worth living. It's no accident that as our culture has increasingly turned its back on God, the suicide rate has gone up. When you remove God from the picture, the options for meaning and purpose are slim to none.

The English philosopher Bertrand Russell was an avowed atheist, but at least he was intellectually honest. He admitted that if you don't believe in God, there are severe consequences. He said, "Unless you assume a God, the question about life's purpose is meaningless."[12] The conclusion is this: If there's no God, then you're just a random accident, a freak of the evolutionary chain, a complex germ. If you're not created by God, your life doesn't matter, and there's no significance to it. It makes no difference whether you're a great humanitarian or a sociopathic serial killer. It's all just random chance.

12 Cited in *Philosophical Consolations of Bertrand Russell*, 22.

But we have far better answers than that. God is our Creator, King, and Savior. He is infinitely loving, wise, and powerful, and we find meaning only in Him. Sixteen centuries ago, Augustine put it this way, "You have made us for Yourself, O Lord, and our hearts are restless until they rest in You." Are you resting in God? That can't happen just because you're smart enough to figure it all out. You're not. It can't happen because you're rich enough, strong enough, or anything else enough. We find rest only because Jesus Christ came among us and died the death we deserved to die for our sins. He paid the penalty so we won't have to. That truth—and even more, the experience of this truth—gives us joy, peace, motivation, and yes, rest. And someday, Jesus will come back to inaugurate the new heavens and new earth, an unimaginably glorious eternity for those who know Him. How we live today will shape our experience in the future . . . the entire future.

But today, right now, you were put here for a reason. Do you know what that is? If you do, live it with all your heart. If you don't, keep reading, keep praying, and keep listening. God delights in showing us what we're made for.

So, where are you in the process of recognizing your limitations, carving out space in your schedule, and pruning the good things so you can focus on the better and best? Yeah, we're all "works in progress." The question posed in this chapter about how we make decisions affects every activity, every relationship, and every goal in our lives. If we learn to trust God more than our ability to make life work, we'll find ways to invest in the things that really matter. At the beginning, saying "no" to good things feels awkward and wrong, but soon, we see the multiplied benefits, and it becomes a normal part of living a wise, God-dependent life.

THE MOTIVES QUESTION:

What's driving your decisions?

→| Key principle: Know your why. |←

THINK ABOUT IT:

1) What are some symptoms of "hurry sickness"? Do you suffer from any of them? Explain your answer.
2) Which of the three lies near the beginning of the chapter have you heard come out of your mouth? What did you expect the payoff to be by believing that lie?
3) Is it difficult for you to admit you have limitations? Why or why not?
4) How would regularly pruning your commitments change your pace, your mindset, and your relationships? What are some reasons people neglect pruning?
5) What are some practical, specific ways you can "bring God into the mix"? What difference will it make?
6) Look at your schedule, and take some time to list all of your responsibilities.
7) What's truly important?
8) What seems urgent but may need to be pruned?
9) What's the payoff of staying so busy?
10) What's the payoff of building in more margin?

CHAPTER 2

THE BELIEFS QUESTION: WHO OR WHAT MAKES YOU HAPPY?

You cannot control what happens to you, but you can control your attitude toward what happens to you, and in that, you will be mastering change rather than allowing it to master you.

— Brian Tracy

As I write this chapter, we're in the middle of football season. One of the things that fascinates me is that grown men who are normally rational become unglued when their team scores—and equally unglued when the other team scores. What's that about? It's about what they believe is most important, at least at that moment.

I don't mean to stereotype, but I know some women whose mood, outlook on life, and sense of identity are wrapped up in how they look, especially at certain events like weddings or parties. What can cause such excitement or despair? It's about what they believe is most important, again, at least at that moment. (And to be fair, I know plenty of men who are quite fashion-conscious, and I know women who are just as fanatical in rooting for their teams.)

We're aware of our choices and emotions, but the driving, shaping, unseen force underneath them is our belief system. Cognitive behavioral therapy has been proven effective on a wide range of psychological problems, including depression, family conflicts, and addictions. The core principles are that these problems are based, at least to some degree, on faulty thinking patterns, especially those that have become ingrained patterns in the person's behavior. Better thinking, the therapy asserts, results in a better mood, more positive emotions, and more productive decisions. Our thinking, though, is a reflection of our very powerful, but often hidden, beliefs. Our beliefs, then, determine virtually everything about us.[13]

Psychologist Dr. Bruce H. Lipton explains that our real beliefs are buried so deep that we're usually not aware of them:

> *The major problem is that people are aware of their conscious beliefs and behaviors, but not of subconscious beliefs and behaviors. Most people don't even acknowledge that their subconscious mind is at play, when the fact is that the subconscious mind is a million times more powerful than the conscious mind and that we operate 95 to 99 percent of our lives from subconscious programs.*
>
> *Your subconscious beliefs are working either for you or against you, but the truth is that you are not controlling your life, because your*

13 "What Is Cognitive Behavioral Therapy," *American Psychological Association*, July 2017, https://www.apa.org/ptsd-guideline/patients-and-families/cognitive-behavioral.

subconscious mind supersedes all conscious control. So when you are trying to heal from a conscious level—citing affirmations and telling yourself you're healthy—there may be an invisible subconscious program that's sabotaging you.[14]

Not surprisingly, the Bible has a lot to say about our core beliefs. We often use the word "heart" to mean emotions, like, "He broke my heart," but the Bible uses the term to mean "the seat of reflection," in other words, our deepest, most dearly held convictions about God, ourselves, our purpose, and the people in our lives. For instance, two proverbs tell us, "Above all else, guard your heart, for everything you do flows from it" (Proverbs 4:23, NIV), and "For as he thinks in his heart, so is he" (Proverbs 23:7, NKJV). The heart is just as important in the New Testament. The apostle Paul had some stern words for the waffling believers in Galatia, so he asked them a penetrating question: "Don't you know that when you allow even a little lie into your heart, it can permeate your entire belief system?" (Galatians 5:9). I'm pretty sure he would ask us the same question!

HAPPINESS IS A CHOICE

Another false belief that is widespread among Christian circles today is that we think we deserve for God to make our lives stress-free and happy. We read quotes on social media and listen to people who insist that it's God's primary job to make us happy. When we believe this, our moods are completely dependent on how we perceive life is going, and we're deeply disillusioned when it appears God hasn't come through like we expected.

The faithful men and women in the Bible and throughout church history would be stunned by these expectations. They didn't blame God or other people when times were hard. They concluded that their situations

14 Bruce H. Lipton, PhD, "Epigenetics," 8 Feb. 2012, https://www.brucelipton.com/epigenetics/.

were tests of faith, and they trusted God to use every circumstance for their good and His glory. They chose the truth about God and the fact that we live in a fallen world. They chose to trust Him through good times and bad. They chose to be "rooted and grounded" in the love of God, not their current situations. Of course, the consummate example of this rigorous faith is Jesus. The writer to the Hebrews explained,

> *We look away from the natural realm and we focus our attention and expectation onto Jesus who birthed faith within us and who leads us forward into faith's perfection. His example is this: Because his heart was focused on the joy of knowing that you would be his, he endured the agony of the cross and conquered its humiliation, and now sits exalted at the right hand of the throne of God!*
>
> *So consider carefully how Jesus faced such intense opposition from sinners who opposed their own souls, so that you won't become worn down and cave in under life's pressures.* —Hebrews 12:2-3

Like Jesus, we have to stay resolute and set our gaze on the joy that is before us, knowing that we can find joy even in our difficulties. Our happiness is our choice. Choose joy!

Like Jesus, we have to stay resolute and set our gaze on the joy that is before us, knowing that we can find joy even in our difficulties. Our happiness is our choice. Choose joy!

HOW BELIEFS ARE SHAPED

Today, our beliefs shape our emotions and behaviors, but what in our past shaped our core beliefs? If this were the chicken and the egg, which came first? Our beliefs have been instilled in us in many different ways. When we were young, our relationship with our parents imprinted specific assumptions on our minds and hearts. Some of us were convinced that we were loved, and we internalized the belief that we have value, most people are trustworthy, and love is readily available. But many others grew up in homes that weren't as loving, supportive, and consistent. They concluded they weren't (and probably still aren't) worthy of love, so they developed coping strategies to earn approval and minimize emotional pain.

Early family relationships make us receptive to certain messages and resistant to others. It's like a radio that's tuned to a certain frequency. The message comes through loud and clear, but only on that station. If it's positive, that's wonderful; if it's toxic, it's all we hear all day every day.

We tend to gravitate toward people who are much like our parents. Before you react and accuse me of being crazy, let me explain: For those who have been overlooked, blamed for the family's problems, and been the target of harsh and unfair criticism, it seems inconceivable that we might be drawn to people who are like those who have hurt us, but that's what happens again and again. It's all about familiarity. We learned to cope with our parents and siblings by developing particular skills, and we feel comfortable using those skills in other relationships—even if those people are just as difficult as our families.

Our experiences as adults often reinforce our core beliefs, for good or ill. We interpret good experiences and bad ones through the grid we developed as children.

Our experiences as adults often reinforce our core beliefs, for good or ill. We interpret good experiences and bad ones through the grid we developed as children. We hear the same voices, feel the same feelings, and act the same ways we did when we were young . . . but maybe with a bit more sophistication and discretion.

I have a friend who generally likes dogs, but not German shepherds. He's happy to put his hand out to most dogs as he walks in his neighborhood, but the sight of a German shepherd triggers a surge of anxiety and a flight response. The story is that when he was in college, his mother asked him to take a Christmas present to some family friends. When he arrived and opened the car door, a German shepherd came running around the corner of the house and came straight for him. As it got closer, he could tell the dog didn't have a friendly expression on its face! As the dog lunged for him, he turned quickly enough that the dog bit him on his back through several layers of clothes.

When the dog fell off, it regrouped for another lunge, but my friend stuck his shoe in the dog's mouth. The loud growling of the attack brought the couple's daughter out of the house. She ran to grab the dog and pulled him away. My friend's shoe was chewed up, but that was a small loss compared to what could have happened to his leg or arm or hand or some other part of his body. When I heard the story, his reaction to the sight of German shepherds today made perfect sense. His beliefs had been hardened in concrete by a traumatic experience.

LOVES AND BELIEFS

Our deepest beliefs aren't sterile. They're connected to whom or what we most desire. Centuries ago, Augustine taught that the central problem of mankind is that we have "disordered loves." It's not that we love too much;

"Let not the wise boast of their wisdom or the strong boast of their strength or the rich boast of their riches, but let the one who boasts boast about this: that they have the understanding to know me, that I am the Lord, who exercises kindness, justice and righteousness on earth, for in these I delight," declares the Lord. —Jeremiah 9:23-24 (ESV)

In ancient times, a "boast" was the source of joy, strength, and identity. Do you know anyone who gets their joy, strength, and identity from being smarter than the other people in the room? By being "one-up" in every relationship? Of having more money and possessions than the other people? Sure you do. They're all around us—and we're probably in the same boat, at least to some degree. That's exactly what God explained to Jeremiah. There's nothing wrong with being intelligent, powerful, and rich, unless these are our boasts. If they're gifts, we'll use them to honor God and help people. If they're our boasts, they'll consume us. Through the prophet, God says He is the only one worth our boasting, but we won't become burdened slaves when we put Him first. No, instead we'll experience His kindness, justice, and righteousness. Not a bad swap!

In a commencement address at Kenyon College, novelist David Foster Wallace put his finger on the problem with making secondary things primary:

If you worship money and things—if they are where you tap real meaning in life—then you will never have enough. Never feel you have enough. It's the truth. Worship your own body and beauty and sexual allure and you will always feel ugly, and when time and age start showing, you will die a million deaths before they finally plant you [in the grave]. On one level, we all know this stuff already—it's been codified as myths, proverbs, clichés, bromides, epigrams, parables: the skeleton of every great story. The trick is keeping the truth up front in it's that our loves are in the wrong order. It's perfectly fine to love a care[er], but when it's more important than our families, it causes a world of problems. And it's perfectly fine to love our families, but when we make them the center of our hearts, we put too much of a burden on them to act in ways that make us feel loved and look like great spouses and parents. The only one who deserves to be in the center of our thoughts and affections is God. When we believe He is supremely lovely, worthy, and good, we can love our families well, and we can work with wisdom and excellence. That's "ordered loves."

Pastor and author, Tim Keller, says that when anyone or anything is in God's rightful place in our hearts, it has become an idol. He identifies four primary pursuits that consume many of us: power, pleasure, popularity, and control. In his book, *Counterfeit Gods,* he asked and answered, "What is an idol? It is anything more important to you than God, anything that absorbs your heart and imagination more than God, anything you seek to give you what only God can give." What weight do we put into these secondary things? "A counterfeit god is anything so central and essential to your life that, should you lose it, your life would feel hardly worth living."[15] Only one thing can be ultimately important to us. When we have it, we feel thankful and strong, but if it's not God, those feelings are like an addiction that keep us coming back, needing more and more to get the same feelings, and wrecking the rest of our lives even if we get what we want so badly.

The prophet Jeremiah had a conversation with God that sheds light on what we believe is most important:

This is what the Lord says:

15 Timothy Keller, *Counterfeit Gods* (New York: Penguin, 2009), xvii, xviii.

daily consciousness. Worship power—you will feel weak and afraid, and you will need ever more power over others to keep the fear at bay. Worship your intellect, being seen as smart—you will end up feeling stupid, a fraud, always on the verge of being found out.[16]

It's fascinating that Wallace, who wasn't a Christian as far as I can tell, called our devotion to money and things, beauty, sexual attraction, power, and intelligence "worship." That's our commitment to these things, and, as he points out, it's lethal to our souls and our most important relationships, including our connection with God.

We get a glimpse of mistaken beliefs in the Bible story of the rich young ruler in Luke 18:18-23 (NIV). He came to Jesus and asked, "Good teacher, what must I do to inherit eternal life?" (v. 18). Sounds like a great question, doesn't it? Wouldn't you think Jesus would be thrilled to hear and answer it? But Jesus looked deep into the young man's heart and corrected him:

"Why do you call me good? No one is good—except God alone" (v. 19). Jesus then spelled out several of the commandments. The young man replied, "All these I have kept since I was a boy" (v. 20). Jesus' list of commandments, though, left one out, the first one: "You shall have no other gods before me" (Exodus 20:3, NIV). Jesus put His finger on that one when He told him, "You still lack one thing. Sell everything you have and give to the poor, and you will have treasure in heaven. Then come, follow me" (v. 22). That was it. That was the sticking point. That was the one thing he wasn't willing to give up. "When he heard this, he became very sad, because he was very wealthy" (v. 23).

---

16 "A Speech by the Late David Foster Wallace," *The Guardian*, Guardian News and Media,19 Sept. 2008, http://www.theguardian.com/books/2008/sep/20/fiction.

In this conversation, we see that the young man was blind to his heart's condition. He tried to compensate for hoarding his money by rigorously fulfilling the other commandments, and when his heart was exposed, he experienced the sadness of shame, not the sadness that leads to repentance.

One of our most fundamental and serious problems is our lack of self-awareness. We're thoroughly convinced the way we see events, ourselves, and other people is flawless. Here's a tip: it's not. In fact, we seldom have all the facts, and even if we did, we're predisposed to see things from a perspective that distorts reality, at least to some degree. Our self-perception is often clouded by two opposite factors: pride and fear. We think too much of ourselves or too little. Wisdom is seeing ourselves as deeply flawed (which makes us humble) and dearly loved by God (which gives us security). This enables us to be ruthlessly honest . . . and hopeful that change is possible.

John Maxwell observes that self-awareness is essential if we're going to enjoy the double win. With it, we can make good choices, set priorities, and put the important before the urgent; without it, we stumble through life making decisions that hurt others and leave us feeling empty. Maxwell says that we need to see ourselves from several points of view, and in fact, we have five different identities:

1) You are who you are.
2) You are who you think you are.
3) You are who your family thinks you are.
4) You are who your friends think you are.
5) You are who your acquaintances think you are.[17]

The less we know about ourselves, the more we'll pretend to be something we're not. The better we know ourselves, the more we will be the

17 "The Self-Aware Leader," *John Maxwell Leadership Podcast*, 15 Dec. 2021, https://johnmaxwellleadershippodcast.com/episodes/john-maxwell-the-self-aware-leader.

same with everyone in every situation. That's integrity . . . congruence . . . and sanity.

UNCOVERING OUR TRUE BELIEFS

Thanks to people like Augustine, Keller, Jeremiah, and Wallace, we can begin to see what really matters to us, but make no mistake—peeling off the layers of excuses and self-justification is hard. As Col. Jessup sneered at Lt. Kaffee in *A Few Good Men*, "You can't handle the truth!" In fact, we're naturally predisposed to avoid it. Let's go back to the prophet Jeremiah and hear God speak through him again: "The heart is deceitful above all things and beyond cure. Who can understand it?" (Jeremiah 17:9, NIV). Sometimes I hear people say, "Well, that's your opinion, but I just need to follow my heart." God would say that's not a recipe for success!

Jesus told a parable about the disconnect between what people say and what they really believe. Peter asked Him for an explanation, and He told them:

> *But the things that come out of a person's mouth come from the heart, and these defile them. For out of the heart come evil thoughts—murder, adultery, sexual immorality, theft, false testimony, slander.*
> —Matthew 15:18-19 (NIV)

God has given us some windows on our souls, so we can peer inside and see what's really there: our emotional reactions, our words, and the consequences of our actions.

» Contrary to what some people assume, emotions aren't right or wrong. The pleasant ones point us to the source of all that's good in our lives, and the painful ones (chiefly fear, anger, hurt, and shame) are yellow (or maybe red) blinking lights on the dashboard of our hearts. Even many of the painful ones are absolutely necessary. There's something terribly wrong with us if we're not afraid when a car is speeding toward us or a child is about to fall out of a tree. The apostle Paul commands us to be angry at injustice but to avoid the sin of getting mad just because we can't have everything our own way. Hurt and grief are necessary to overcome loss. Shame is only productive if it leads to repentance if we're at fault, or it leads us to grieve and set boundaries if it's the product of abuse or neglect. These emotions are ways God is calling us to stop for a minute, look inside, and see what's really going on. But don't assume unpleasant feelings are always negative and should be avoided. Many times they're exactly the right response to an injustice or a wound.

» As Jesus said, what comes out of our mouths is a very good indicator of what's in our hearts. He uses another metaphor about trees and says that a good tree produces good fruit and a bad tree produces bad fruit. The determining factor, then, isn't the fruit but the health of the tree. It's the same with us. What comes out of your mouth in a given day? Is it gratitude, hope, encouragement, and blessings? Or is it blaming others, vicious self-criticism, self-pity, bitterness, and negativity? I would guess that most of us are a mixed bag, so let me ask it this way: In which direction is the needle moving?

» Certainly, we sometimes experience heartaches that aren't connected with our choices. We may eat well, exercise, and take care of our bodies, but we can still get cancer or another dreaded disease. We may have gotten a huge discount on our car insurance because we're such safe drivers, but we get rear-ended by someone who is not paying attention because they're looking at their phone. You get the picture. So it's not productive to assume that all suffering has a direct link to our choices, but a lot of it has.

If we believe life is all about pleasure, we'll make financial, time, and relationship decisions that give us a good time, but we'll inevitably pay a steep price. If we believe we're unattractive, we'll look in the mirror a hundred times a day to see if we look better, or more times than not, despise ourselves for not looking better. The harsh voice of the inner critic is enough of a consequence. If we believe we're only valuable if we're on top, in charge, and in control of everyone and everything, we'll live in constant fear of losing our position, and we'll crave power and control at the expense of others.

We're quite skilled in avoiding the truth about our hearts, and we've come up with a lot of creative ways to muddy the waters. Many of us have "destination disease": we excuse our inappropriate focus on money, titles, prestige, and power by insisting, "When I get to that point in my life, I'll have better priorities." Others are incredibly skilled at pointing the finger at someone else (anyone else!). We blame our boss, our parents, our spouse, our kids, the government, a politician, and others for making us miserable, and we feel completely justified in complaining . . . a lot! I've talked to quite a few couples who tell me they're not compatible any longer. That's why they argue all the time. Their marriages started as the ideal, then turned to an ordeal, and now they're looking for a new deal!

We say we believe the Bible, but do we? It says that maturity and wisdom come through suffering, so even though suffering is unpleasant, it's the graduate school of the Christian life.

Our happiness isn't in the hands of someone else. It's all about how we choose to interpret life's events and challenges. We say we believe the Bible, but do we? It says that maturity and wisdom come through suffering, so even though suffering is unpleasant, it's the graduate school of the Christian life. Do we believe in the sovereignty, goodness, and wisdom of God? If we do, we'll pour out our hearts to Him, clinging to Him in the hard times, and thanking Him all the time because we're convinced that He always has our good in mind.

MIND CONTROL

No, I'm not suggesting some kind of New Age mysticism. The Bible gives clear directions for reinforcing our good and godly beliefs. In the apostle Paul's second letter to the Corinthians, he explained that it's a battle, actually siege warfare, to get control of our thoughts:

> *For though we live in the world, we do not wage war as the world does. The weapons we fight with are not the weapons of the world. On the contrary, they have divine power to demolish strongholds. We demolish arguments and every pretension that sets itself up against the knowledge of God, and we take captive every thought to make it obedient to Christ.* —2 Corinthians 10:3-5 (NIV)

Those deeply ingrained false beliefs about God, ourselves, and the way life ought to go are strongholds, and they don't go away easily. We have to fight, demolish them, and replace them with God's truth. How often? Whatever it takes, as often as it takes. A friend recommends writing an encouraging passage of scripture on a card or a sticky note and having it handy throughout the day. He says he reads his about twenty times a day. Like I said: "Whatever it takes."

Can we actually choose our thoughts, so they reshape and reinforce our beliefs? Absolutely. The apostle Paul wrote the Philippians,

> *Finally, brothers and sisters, whatever is true, whatever is noble, whatever is right, whatever is pure, whatever is lovely, whatever is admirable—if anything is excellent or praiseworthy—think about such things. Whatever you have learned or received or heard from me, or seen in me—put it into practice. And the God of peace will be with you."* —Philippians 4:8-9

This passage isn't in a vacuum. Paul had earlier described the grace and greatness of Jesus, so here he's reminding us: Jesus is truth. He is noble. His ways are right. He is pure, lovely, excellent, and worthy of praise. If we want our core beliefs to change, we need to camp out in the goodness and greatness of Jesus Christ. Then we'll think more positively and honestly, we'll speak with more grace, and we'll live in ways that honor God and bless the people around us.

FOUR HABITS

Is happiness really a choice? Can we experience the double win at home and at work instead of feeling frustrated and pressured all the time? Yes, but we need to acquire a set of habits that enable us to choose happiness no matter what the circumstances may be. Life throws us curveballs, especially when we're expecting something easy to come our way. The four most common killjoys we face are pain, people, pressures, and problems.

The four most common killjoys we face are pain, people, pressures, and problems.

To find happiness even in times of trouble . . .

1) Shift your perspective.

   The fact that we can't see what God is doing behind the scenes doesn't mean He's not working for our good all the time. He even uses our mistakes and sins if we'll trust Him. In his classic book, *Knowing God*, author and professor J. I. Packer explains:

   > *This is what all the work of grace aims at—an ever deeper knowledge of God, and an ever closer fellowship with Him. Grace is God drawing us sinners closer and closer to Himself. How does God in grace prosecute this purpose? Not by shielding us from assault by the world, the flesh, and the devil, nor by protecting us from burdensome and frustrating circumstances, nor yet by shielding us from troubles created by our own temperament and psychology; but rather by exposing us to all these things, so as to overwhelm us with a sense of our own inadequacy, and to drive us to cling to Him more closely. This is the ultimate reason, from our standpoint, why God fills our lives with troubles and perplexities of one sort and another—it is to ensure that we shall learn to hold Him fast. . . .*[18]

18 J. I. Packer, *Knowing God* (Downers Grove, IL: InterVarsity Press, 1973), 226-228.

2) Don't let others highjack your happiness.

The apostle Paul's letter to the Philippians is a thank you note to people who have encouraged and supported him. In the first chapter, he explains that their love is in stark contrast to some people who have stood against him. Some are fierce critics, some are competitors, and still others are conspirators who want to rub it in that he's in prison for his faith in Jesus.

Would you agree that few things can rob your happiness faster than being criticized? When you're criticized at work, by friends, or by neighbors, your stomach starts churning. Why? Because you want to be liked and loved. You want others' approval and affirmation. But Paul rose above all that. He explained, "But whether or not their motives are pure, the fact remains that the message about Christ is being preached; so I rejoice. I will continue to rejoice no matter what" (Philippians 1:18, NIV).

Over the past thirty years, I have been misunderstood, betrayed, and criticized. My dad used to say, "If you want to avoid criticism, say nothing, do nothing, and be nothing." It's impossible to please everyone and make everyone happy. I love what Steve Jobs once said: "If you want to make everyone happy, don't be a leader, sell ice cream!" We can't let the devil use other people's fickleness and the fiery arrows they shoot to rob us of our happiness. The apostle Paul felt the same way. He remarked, "Be fearless, no matter who opposes you. It will be a sign to them of their downfall, and that God is with you, and that he will save you" (Philippians 1:28, TLB). At the end of the day, we can't control what everybody says, believes, or thinks about us. Our aim is to live for an audience of ONE.

3) Worry less and trust God more.

When things are falling apart in my world, I don't try to put them back together on my own. I've learned to let God help me put the pieces of life back together. This is the faith factor. When you're going through a problem, you've got two options: you can worship, or you can worry, but you can't do both. If you worshiped more, you'd have a whole lot less to worry about. You can pray, or you can panic. Those are the options you've got. It's your choice to rejoice.

4) Stay focused on your purpose, not your problem.

Even though the apostle Paul was old by the time he wrote to the Philippians, and he was in prison awaiting execution, he didn't whine and complain. His heart was riveted on his God-given purpose, and nothing could stop him from accomplishing everything God had given him to do.

Viktor Frankl was a Jewish psychiatrist who was captured and sent to the Nazi concentration camp at Theresienstadt, and later to Auschwitz. The rest of his family was gassed and cremated, and he watched other prisoners slowly succumb to the devastation of starvation and dehumanization inflicted by the guards. If anyone had a reason to be consumed by problems it was these ghosts of men. However, in the middle of this trauma, Frankl focused on his last remaining choice. In his book, *Man's Search for Meaning,* he wrote, "Everything can be taken from a man but one thing: the last of human freedoms—to choose one's attitude in any given set of circumstances, to choose one's own way."[19]

If he could keep his perspective there, you and I can keep ours wherever we are.

---

19 Viktor Frankl, *Man's Search for Meaning* (London: Ebury Publishing, 1946), 66.

The reason why most people are miserable is because they think that happiness comes from self-gratification. "If I just have more nice things, if I can enjoy more pleasures, if I can attain a higher position, if I get more sex, salary, or status, I'll be happier." That doesn't work. Actually, self-gratification isn't the way to happiness. The way to happiness is self-sacrifice. The apostle Paul says, in effect, "The reason I'm happy is because as long as I'm alive, I'm giving my life away to help others."

Are you living a self-directed life or a Christ-directed life? Are you living for the temporary or the eternal? If you're living for yourself, and living for the temporary things of this world, I'm quite sure of this: you're not very happy. Happiness comes from serving others—giving your life away. Until you understand that fact, you're not going to be happy. Winston Churchill once said, "You make a living by what you get; you make a life by what you give." Similarly, the apostle Paul wrote in Philippians 1:21 (author paraphrase), "For me, to live is Christ." That's all that mattered to him. Other things could be taken away, rot, get stolen, or be consumed, but Christ is always more than we could ever imagine. Choose Him at home and at work. He alone is the source of our happiness.

THE BELIEFS QUESTION:

Who or what makes you happy?

→| Key principle: Happiness is a choice. |←

THINK ABOUT IT:

1) Think back over the course of your life, and especially your childhood and pivotal events. Make a list of the most significant events.
2) How did these things shape your beliefs about your value, your safety, your potential, and your competence?
3) Think about people in the news and maybe some you know (Write in code if that person is sitting near you!), and try to identify what they boast in?
4) Do you think the term "idolatry" or "counterfeit gods" is too harsh to describe misplaced priorities? Explain your answer.
5) Reflect on your words, your emotions, and the consequences of your choices over the past couple of days. What deep beliefs do they uncover?
6) What are some practical steps you can take to wage siege warfare against your false beliefs and drive the truth about Jesus deep into your mind and heart? What difference will it make?
7) What can you do to develop each of the four habits described in this chapter?

» Shift your perspective.

» Don't let others highjack your happiness.

» Worry less and trust God more.

» Stay focused on your purpose, not your problem.

CHAPTER 3

THE DREAM QUESTION: WHAT DOES YOUR FUTURE LOOK LIKE?

A person who has a dream knows what he is willing to give up in order to go up.
—John C. Maxwell

Several years ago, Michelle and I took a trip with our son, Luke, to Lynchburg, Virginia. Since we had a solid ten-and-a-half hours of drive time ahead of us, we decided to get an early start, so we could get a jump on the morning traffic. We left the house around 6:00 a.m., which would put us in Lynchburg early enough to have dinner with our daughter, Ashlyn. Since following directions isn't exactly my strong suit (at least according to Michelle), I told her I knew how to get to Lynchburg without the GPS. After about five hours of driving, we crossed into

Alabama, and suddenly, we all knew something was wrong. (In fact, I had been sensing it for quite a while, but I refused to say anything. I wanted Michelle and Luke to believe I was in total control.)

Michelle picked up her phone, opened the GPS app, and quickly realized we were headed in the wrong direction. We were on the route to Birmingham, which is where our daughter Becca and her husband, Daniel, live. Michelle reminded me again that I'm not very good at directions, and Luke piled on. I apologized, opened the GPS app on my phone, and put in the correct address to Ashlyn's house. Needless to say, we didn't make it to Lynchburg in time to have dinner with her, but we had a great midnight snack! The three of us knew where we wanted to go, but we (I) took the wrong path. It can happen to any of us.

Author and pastor Andy Stanley observes, "Direction, not intention, determines your destination."[20] Let me ask you: Where are you going? Where is your family going spiritually, morally, relationally, financially? Are you using your God-given imagination to envision your future?

REVISED DEFINITION

Almost invariably when we talk about the future, especially "an ideal future," we imagine "having arrived" at a heaven-on-earth stage of ease and plenty. If we pay attention to the not-so-subtle message behind every commercial, we'll see that they promise their product or service won't just clean our teeth, taste good, or be a good investment; it will fulfill our deepest desires! (No wonder they're so powerful.) I want to offer a fairly radical redefinition: *It's all about the journey, not the destination.* Our experiences and the lessons we learn along the path of life are more important and transformative than arriving at a desired destination. We're happier,

---

20 Andy Stanley, *The Principle of the Path* (Nashville: Thomas Nelson, 2008), 44.

we're more fulfilled, and we make more of a difference when we see every moment as a gift from God to be used to have an impact on those around us. This means that the full range of human experiences, from the highest joys to the deepest grief, can effectively draw us closer to God and the people we love . . . but only when we see them that way. Heartaches are often God's shout or whisper to get our attention, so He can redirect us, deepen our faith, and teach us life's most important lessons.

Our dreams of the future are vital, but they need to be in line with God's purposes.

Our dreams of the future are vital, but they need to be in line with God's purposes. He doesn't plan for us to endure drudgery until we get to a point, many years from now, when life suddenly works out and makes sense. He wants us to have a different dream: that He will infuse every step in the path forward with meaning, hope, and purpose. Life's a journey, not a destination.

Let me offer some recommendations to define the dream, write it down, and make it a reality.

DEFINE THE DREAM

The leaders of virtually every corporation, nonprofit organization, and church have taken time to define (and refine) their mission and vision. The mission is why you exist, your purpose; the vision describes where you're going, your direction. When these are clear and compelling, people get up every day with deeper motivation than just making money or finishing a task. They're passionately committed to making a difference and impacting lives. But these powerful tools aren't just for organizations; they're for individuals, couples, and families too. Each of us needs to take the time to define our why and our where.

Unfortunately, we often settle for a pale imitation of the real thing. For instance . . .

» We daydream about winning the lottery, being famous, or some other distraction from reality.

» We have wild ideas with no firm grasp of reality and no workable strategy.

» On the other end of the spectrum, we're paralyzed by worry and fear of the unknown.

» We don't think and dream for ourselves. Instead, we adopt someone else's dream.

» We imagine finding just the right romantic partner who will make us happy and fulfill our fantasies.

» We assume the next step up the organizational ladder, recognition, or a raise will bring real joy.

» We spend countless hours online looking at a new boat, car, house, kitchen, or something else that promises to make us happy.

In *Put Your Dream to the Test,* John C. Maxwell notes,

> *A dream is an inspiring picture of the future that energizes your mind, will, and emotions, empowering you to do everything you can to achieve it. A dream worth pursuing is a picture and blueprint of a person's purpose and potential.*[21]

---

21 John C. Maxwell, *Put Your Dream to the Test* (Nashville: Thomas Nelson, 2011), xiii.

All of us are craftsmen. God has given us talents and skills, and He has put resources in our hands (or within reach) to do what He has called us to do. In the vast majority of cases, we follow our why to our where with little notoriety, but those who love us notice. We quietly and effectively construct a family and friendships that are beautiful and meaningful.

A vision may stretch us to be more and do more, but as we saw earlier, we need to recognize our limitations. My dream isn't to play on the PGA Tour. I don't have the talents to do that. But God has given me a mission and vision for families across America to build strong, healthy relationships. As a pastor, I want the same thing for the people in our church. In fact, as I mentioned in the introductory chapter, I can only serve others well as a pastor if my own marriage and family life are strong, loving, and healthy. That's the journey we're on all day every day.

When our family was younger, some mentors we greatly admired encouraged us to write down our purpose and vision as a family and establish a set of core values for our home. They shared how valuable it had been to them when they were raising their kids and how it helped them stay centered on what's most important. We decided to take them up on their advice. Here's what we came up with:

The Gage family's purpose is to live, learn, laugh, and love. This means we . . .

» Live passionately: We live each day to its fullest, living without regrets.

» Learn: We keep growing and pay attention to our successes and failures. Failure is never final.

» Laugh: We have fun. We don't take ourselves too seriously. We want to make others smile.

» Love unconditionally: We want to love people the way God loves us.

We also defined a set of core values for our family. These became the nonnegotiables when it came to the qualities and characteristics that were important to us and how we wanted to be known as a family. Our core values are character, loyalty, faith, integrity, honesty, purity, and generosity. We used these to serve as guardrails and guideposts to keep us on track and to help us make wise decisions.

We also chose a Bible verse to serve as a theme for our family:

> *Don't copy the behavior and customs of this world, but let God transform you into a new person by changing the way you think. Then you will learn to know God's will for you, which is good and pleasing and perfect.* —Romans 12:2 (NLT)

From this verse in the Bible we were inspired to write a vision statement:

> *Our vision is to be a family that lives differently from the norm by standing up and standing out for Jesus, so we can win others to Christ and continue our family's legacy of faith for generations to come.*

To reinforce our purpose, and vision we had a stencil made in cursive font and put it above our door in the home to serve as a constant reminder to what we wanted to be known for as a family: "But as for me and my family, we will serve the LORD" (Joshua 24:15, NLT).

Please don't misunderstand why I am sharing all of this with you. My intent isn't to try to impress you or make it appear that we had it all together and lived like a bunch of monks, priests, and nuns. In fact, we were far from the perfect family (and still are). However, establishing these statements of faith and family declarations helped serve as a visual reminder of who we were striving to become as a family. The declarations also helped us stay centered and grounded. Knowing who we were striving to become kept us from getting distracted from what was most important.

It also helped us establish a family culture by defining what type of behaviors were acceptable and unacceptable. When one of our children displayed attitudes and behaviors that were inconsistent with our vision, purpose, and core values, we could point them to what we agreed to as a family. This always provided a starting point for all discussions with our children when they were younger, and I'll tell you, it was priceless!

This is why it's so important to write down your vision, purpose, and values for your life, marriage, and family. I realize writing your vision and values doesn't guarantee everything will go smoothly, and everyone will be on board all the time. However, not writing these things increases the chances of you NOT fulfilling your desired future spiritually, relationally, and morally. Regardless of your situation—nuclear family, single parent, blended family—make a commitment to articulate and capture what your hopes, dreams, desires, and expectations are for your family by putting it in writing.

If companies, businesses, and academic institutions can have purpose and vision statements, why can't we have them for our marriages and families? The family is the first institution God created. It's the foundation of all societies, no matter the nation or politics. Over the years, our family has revised and refined our vision and values. Like us, they're always works in progress, but I wanted to include our family's to serve as an example, give you some ideas, and to encourage you as you consider your own.

WRITE IT DOWN

The prophet Habakkuk reported God's answer to a question:

"Write down the revelation and make it plain on tablets so that a herald may run with it. For the revelation awaits an appointed time; it

speaks of the end and will not prove false. Though it linger, wait for it; it will certainly come and will not delay." —Habakkuk 2:2-3 (NIV)

Writing is a vital part in defining, articulating, and living out our God-given purpose. In an article in *Forbes*, Mark Murphy reports that people who describe or use pictures to illuminate their goals are 1.2 to 1.4 times as likely to accomplish them. He explains that writing down our goals is effective in two important ways:

Writing things down happens on two levels: external storage and encoding. External storage is easy to explain: you're storing the information contained in your goal in a location (e.g. a diary or journal) that's very easy to access and review at any time. You could type up your family vision and put it in a frame in your office, or write it on a piece of paper to put on your refrigerator. It doesn't take a neuroscientist to explain that you'll remember something much better if you're staring at a visual cue to remind you every single day. Be creative and have fun with it!

But there's another deeper phenomenon happening: encoding. Encoding is the biological process by which the things we perceive travel to our brain's hippocampus where they're analyzed. From there, decisions are made about what gets stored in our long-term memory and, in turn, what gets discarded. Writing improves that encoding process. In other words, when you write it down it has a much greater chance of being remembered.[22]

Beyond neuroscience, I've encouraged people to write their goals, purpose, and vision because writing has multiple benefits:

---

22 Mark Murphy, "Neuroscience Explains Why You Need to Write Down Your Goals If You Actually Want to Achieve Them," *Forbes*, 15 Apr. 2018, https://www.forbes.com/sites/markmurphy/2018/04/15/neuroscience-explains-why-you-need-to-write-down-your-goals-if-you-actually-want-to-achieve-them/?sh=3f100f6d7905.

- » It forces us to clarify what we really want.
- » It motivates us to take action.
- » It provides a filter to assess other opportunities.
- » It helps us overcome hindrances and resistance.
- » It enables us to see and celebrate progress.

[Go to our website at thewinningfamily.com to download a worksheet. It will help you define and articulate your family's purpose and vision.]

Make Your Dream a Reality

A few of us are naturally gifted at details and follow-through, but most of us need a workable, clear plan if we want to make progress in experiencing the double win at home and at work. To make your dreams become real, consider these steps:

1) Believe in yourself.

   As you look at the journey you've written about, you may feel more than a twinge of self-doubt, but focus on what you bring to the table. You have experience, talents, and other resources. Write down the things you've attempted before and found success with. That's your track record. Don't accept your life as it is because it's the hand you've been dealt, and don't believe that life is as good as it's going to get. It's your responsibility to become everything that you are capable of becoming, not only for your benefit but also everyone else's.

2) Believe in your dream.

   Your journey will have a profoundly positive impact on the people you love. Keep the dream alive by imagining what difference it will make to have clear direction for your marriage and family, and take the necessary steps along the way.

3) Set benchmarks.

Any significant trip involves stops to refuel the car and the people inside it. As you think about the journey, what progress can you expect in three months, six months, a year, five years, and many more years in the future? These markers remind you that you're making progress, so they reinforce your why and your where.

Find the balance of reaching for the stars and being rigorously realistic.

Most of us drift to one end or the other, so you may need some help finding the right balance. The people around you may not be cut from the same cloth, so don't assume they're as aggressive or as cautious as you are when it comes to achieving your goals.

4) Find a partner.

Your spouse, kids, or trusted friend are built-in accountability partners. Bounce ideas off them, ask for their feedback, and talk through details with them. It's important to engage them in every step of the process. It's their journey, too!

5) Be persistent.

On every road trip, we encounter potholes, detours, delays, and other problems. It's the same in life's journey. Expect them, prepare for them as best you can, and don't panic when they happen. We may face pushback from people who don't understand our dreams . . . and some of those people may live under our roofs! One of the marks of maturity is the ability to graciously press ahead in difficult times. Some experts observe that many people experience "the death of a dream," but that death becomes the source of a new way of pursuing the dream, so it's followed by a resurrection that's even better than when it was originally conceived.

6) Don't compare yourself or your dream to anyone else.

    Comparison is entirely normal . . . and absolutely lethal! When our eyes are on someone else, they aren't where they should be. You may have heard of the 18/40/60 Rule: When you're 18, you worry about what everybody else is thinking about you. When you're 40, you don't care what others think about you. When you're 60, you realize no one has been thinking about you all along!

7) Celebrate often and well.

    One of the most effective ways to stay on track with any goal is to celebrate incremental successes. If we wait until we arrive at the destination, we will have missed countless opportunities to say, "Hey, look how far we've come! Isn't that amazing! I can't wait to see what's coming next."

"THANKS, I NEEDED THAT!"

Years ago, a commercial for Mennen Skin Bracer, a men's shaving lotion, showed a man slapping it on his face. Suddenly, his sleepy expression turns wide-eyed, and he remarks, "Thanks, I needed that!" As I've talked to singles and couples about the benefits of pairing a dream with a plan, many have responded the same way. Most of us need a jolt to get us moving, to renew our passion for life, and to dream of a fabulous journey for us and our families. Without that wake-up call, we drift through life, trying to hang on to small dreams, and hoping they'll give us the joy, love, and fulfillment we crave.

The apostle Paul gave a similar wake-up call to the Ephesians:

> *Wake up from your sleep, Climb out of your coffins; Christ will show you the light! So watch your step. Use your head. Make the most of every chance you get. These are desperate times! Don't live carelessly,*

unthinkingly. Make sure you understand what the Master wants.
—Ephesians 5:14-17 (MSG)

In his book *The Compound Effect,* Darren Hardy describes the importance of making course corrections when we drift, even slightly, from our desired course. He uses the illustration of a plane traveling from Los Angeles to New York City:

If the nose of the plane is pointed only 1 percent off course during flight—almost an invisible adjustment when the plane's sitting on the tarmac in Los Angeles—it will ultimately end up 150 miles off course, arriving either upstate in Albany or in Dover, Delaware.[23]

This illustration emphasizes how important it is for us to revisit our dreams and goals on a regular basis. A single decision, which doesn't look like much in the moment, can ultimately lead us miles off course from our goals and the life we desire. The late Zig Ziglar once said, "When obstacles arise, you change your direction to reach your goal. You do not change your decision to get there."[24]

As we think, pray, and plan for our journey, we need to hold firm to the decision of what could be and should be when it comes to our family, career, health, finances, or whatever we're striving to achieve.

TOO LATE?

More than a few people have read this chapter, and instead of feeling inspired, they feel deflated. They've concluded, *Yeah, other people can trust God for a wonderful journey to a terrific destination, but not me. I've blown it too badly. (Or I've been hurt too badly.) It's too late for me.*

---

23 Darren Hardy, *The Compound Effect* (Philadelphia: Vanguard Press, 2011), 60.
24 Zig Ziglar, "Obstacles and Goals," *Ziglar Inc*, 28 Mar. 2017, https://www.ziglar.com/quotes/obstacles-and-goals/.

Let me assure you, it's never too late. Sure, we bring our wounds and scars with us on the trip, but God can weave our heartaches into a new, beautiful fabric. How do people become wise? By having to trust God for wisdom in their dire situations. How do they learn to love? When they felt unloved and unlovable, someone stepped in to love them just the same. How do they find hope? By seeing God provide for them when life seemed hopeless. How do they appreciate forgiveness? By being ruthlessly honest about their sins and trusting God to cleanse them.

Some of the most inspiring stories I've ever heard are told by people who have had it rough—really rough, and they trusted God to make something beautiful out of the mess. The apostle Paul wrote to the Christians in Philippi:

> *But one thing I do: Forgetting what is behind and straining toward what is ahead, I press on toward the goal to win the prize for which God has called me heavenward in Christ Jesus.* —Philippians 3:13-14 (NIV)

We may have lost hope because we're victims of other people's sins, or we may have lost hope because we've made foolish, selfish decisions. Psalm 107 (NIV) gives us four scenarios of people in trouble. The first group "wandered in wastelands" (v. 4); the second group was in prison "because they rebelled against God's commands and despised the plans of the Most High" (v. 11); the third group was rebellious and "suffered affliction because of their iniquities" (v. 17); and the fourth group was made up of sailors who encountered a terrible storm. The common response of all of them was that "they cried out to the Lord in their trouble" (vv. 6, 13, 19, and 28). What happened? In the same verses they cried, "He saved them from their distress." The point is that no matter the cause of our problems, we can cry out to God for help.

No matter who you are, no matter what you've done, no matter how far you feel from God, it's never too late to fulfill God's purpose for you. If you have a pulse, you have a purpose.

No one is beyond the love, grace, and power of God. No one is too far gone. No one has been written off by God. In fact, it's obvious from the lessons we learn in the Bible that God takes special delight in turning lives around, rescuing those who seem hopelessly lost, and giving those who have royally messed up their lives a new sense of purpose. If that's you, you're in good company. No matter who you are, no matter what you've done, no matter how far you feel from God, it's never too late to fulfill God's purpose for you. If you have a pulse, you have a purpose.

THE DREAM QUESTION:

What does the ideal future look like?

Key principle: Life's a journey, not a destination.

THINK ABOUT IT:

1) What are the gifts, talents, and other resources God has put in your hands?
2) If you were God, how would you use a person like you?

3) Why is it important to see the journey as the mission, not just the destination?
4) Which of the misguided dreams and distractions have gotten people you know off track? (If that person is sitting next to you, use hieroglyphics!)
5) What have been the consequences in that person's life and relationships?
6) How hard is it for you to find the balance of reaching for the stars and being rigorously realistic?
7) Do you need a wake-up call? Why or why not?

PART 2

REFOCUS

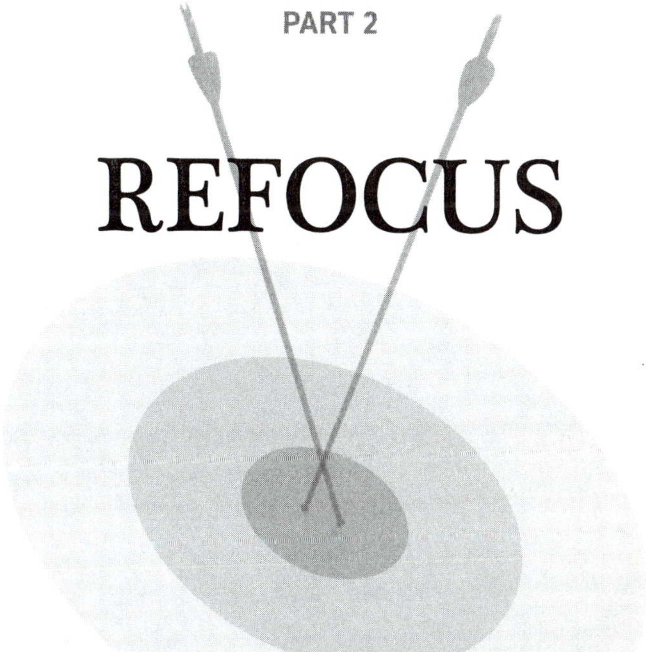

CHAPTER 4

THE VALUES QUESTION: WHAT DO YOU WANT TO BE KNOWN FOR?

Personable leads to remarkable. Remarkable leads to memorable.

—Jeff Henderson

Even during a global pandemic in 2021, the iconic fast food restaurant, Chick-fil-A, took in over $15 billion in revenue. When most restaurants struggled to stay open, Chick-fil-A continued to expand their locations. One of my dear friends is a Chick-fil-A owner.

I sat down with him over lunch one day and asked him what made the company so wildly successful compared to other fast-food franchises. He said,

Rodney, it's simple. It's our core values. The culture of our company and each individual store embodies three key values: operational excellence, second-mile service, and emotional connection. We have one simple goal for our customers. We aim to deliver a remarkable experience.

My experience supports his conclusions: I've been to Chick-fil-A restaurants all across the country, and every one of them is spot-on when it comes to delivering a remarkable experience. They're always efficient, no matter how long the line is, and the inside is always clean (which shows their operational excellence). If you dine in, they offer to pick up your tray, get you a free refill, or serve you in any other way. And they will even bring the food to you if you have to wait (which is second-mile service). The employees ask you how your day is going, give you a friendly smile, and say, "Thank you" (cementing an emotional connection). No wonder they have such loyal customers. They deliver a remarkable experience that's driven by their corporate values.

I believe one of the greatest crisis we face in society today is a values crisis. Some people assume that any talk about values is relegated to fairly meaningless conversations in the C-suites of large corporations. I beg to differ. Carefully identified, sifted, and articulated values are the foundation of every relationship—in marriages, parenting, friendships, churches, and work. But the concept often seems vague, which makes it uninspiring. I believe we can fix that. In fact, we have to fix that!

Let's begin with some definitions and descriptions. To value something means to see it as important and useful, to hold it in high regard. It's often used to identify the principles, beliefs, and standards of an individual or social group, like a family, a church, or a company.[25] Most of us have picked up our values by osmosis—we absorbed whatever was in the atmosphere around us, but a few of us have taken the time to think deeply

25 Some sources of these definitions are Lexico.com, vocabulary.com, and the *Collins English Dictionary*.

about what's most important. I've found it helpful to ask myself a set of penetrating questions:

» What do I want to be known for?
» What's important in our marriage?
» What beliefs and lifestyle do I want to impart to my children (and grandchildren)?
» What influence do I want to have on the people around me (neighbors, friends, and colleagues)?
» How can I live so that God will one day say to me, "Well done, good and faithful servant. Enter into the joy of your master" (Matthew 25:21, ESV)?

If these questions are really easy for you to answer, I would guess that you haven't thought about them enough! If you take shortcuts to adopt someone else's values, they probably won't last when heartaches and difficulties hit. And if you say you value everything, that means you really don't even value your values enough to take the time to consider what you want to be known for. Some people have very definite values in their careers, but they coast at home, and others are just the opposite. To be coherent, we need values that operate wherever we go.

Too often, people assume their spiritual lives are active for an hour on Sunday morning but not for the rest of the week. That's a complete misunderstanding of what it means to be a follower of Christ! We belong to Him all day every day, and we represent Him to everyone we meet. In *The Call*, Os Guinness explains the full range of what it means to belong to God:

> *Calling is the truth that God calls us to himself so decisively that everything we are, everything we do, and everything we have is invested*

with a special devotion and dynamism lived out as a response to his summons and service.[26]

Everything. Everything. Everything. From the bedroom to the boardroom, from the practice field to the ballet recital, from the cradle to the grave, we're partners with the Creator, Savior, and King in the greatest enterprise the world has ever known: making God's kingdom a present reality, if only in part, on earth.

Everything. Everything. Everything. From the bedroom to the boardroom, from the practice field to the ballet recital, from the cradle to the grave, we're partners with the Creator, Savior, and King in the greatest enterprise the world has ever known: making God's kingdom a present reality, if only in part, on earth.

SUCCESS OR SIGNIFICANCE?

In our world, people are known for their accomplishments. It's true in sports, business, art, finances, the military, and every other field. But increasingly, people are seeing the emptiness of this emphasis; they're learning to value significance more than success. Some who have made a lot of money realize that giving and serving others is worth far more than a fatter investment portfolio. And some who have acquired enormous

26 Os Guinness, *The Call* (Nashville: Thomas Nelson, 2003), 5.

power in a company or the culture realize the rat race is eating them alive, so they've turned a corner to use their power to care for people.

Our character, defined by our values, determines our impact on the people around us.

Our character, defined by our values, determines our impact on the people around us. Every day (and in fact, every minute), we have a choice to pursue success defined by power, possessions, and prestige . . . or to pursue God's purpose for us. After describing the wonders of God's grace in his letter to the Romans, the apostle Paul encouraged them (and us) to let that grace transform our values:

> *Beloved friends, what should be our proper response to God's marvelous mercies? To surrender yourselves to God to be his sacred, living sacrifices. And live in holiness, experiencing all that delights his heart. For this becomes your genuine expression of worship. Stop imitating the ideals and opinions of the culture around you, but be inwardly transformed by the Holy Spirit through a total reformation of how you think. This will empower you to discern God's will as you live a beautiful life, satisfying and perfect in his eye.* —Romans 12:1-2

Success satisfies for a moment, and then we have to get more to get the same feeling. But significance fills our souls with joy, confidence, and gratitude. Choose significance.

CONTRASTS

Professor and author N. T. Wright has observed that people learn by contrasts: Not this but that.

Jesus was the consummate teacher, and He often used contrasts in His messages. In the last section of His most famous message, The Sermon on the Mount, He pointed to two gates (narrow and wide), two roads (leading to destruction or eternal life), two trees (bearing good fruit and bad), and two houses with different foundations (one that stands strong in storms and the other that doesn't). We often think of these contrasts as "good and evil," but a more careful look back into the sermon suggests a richer understanding. Earlier, Jesus had contrasted two kinds of people who pray, but He didn't say one prays and the other doesn't. He says one prays selfishly and the other prays humbly. He makes the same point with giving and fasting. What does all this mean? Let's look more closely at the last duo and draw some conclusions.

> *"Everyone who hears my teaching and applies it to his life can be compared to a wise man who built his house on an unshakable foundation. When the rains fell and the flood came, with fierce winds beating upon his house, it stood firm because of its strong foundation.*
>
> *"But everyone who hears my teaching and does not apply it to his life can be compared to a foolish man who built his house on sand. When it rained and rained and the flood came, with wind and waves beating upon his house, it collapsed and was swept away."*
>
> *By the time Jesus finished speaking, the crowds were awestruck by his teaching, because his words carried such great authority, quite unlike the religious scholars.* —Matthew 7:24-29

Jesus was saying that it's possible to look good and godly on the outside but go through the wrong gate, take the wrong road, bear shriveled fruit, and be devastated by the storms of life instead of standing strong. The contrasts are between self-effort and trust in God, self-promotion and humble gratitude, independence and dependence—and He's talking about people who have come to hear Him speak, like those who come to church!

So, the values of God's kingdom aren't only external. That's not enough. They have to be rooted in our hearts, so our outside matches our inside.

So, the values of God's kingdom aren't only external. That's not enough. They have to be rooted in our hearts, so our outside matches our inside.

ADOPTING GOD'S VALUES

From the day our ancestors were ushered out of the Garden of Eden, we've struggled to find the right source of our values. Barna participated with Impact 360 Institute to study the beliefs of Generation Z, people born between 1999 and 2015, but for the sake of this study, people who were between 13 and 18 years old. Among the many surprises, they found:

» Only 9% were classified as "engaged Christians." Almost twice as many, 16%, are "unchurched Christians."

» Family isn't a major priority. "Personal achievement, whether educational or professional (43%), and hobbies and pastimes (42%) are more central to Gen Z's identity than family background/upbringing (34%). By comparison, all other generations rank family at the top."

» A majority "want to finish their education (66%), start a career (66%) and become financially independent (65%) by age 30, while only one in five wants to get married by then (20%)."[27]

» Only 4% have a biblical worldview.

Their study concludes, "Today's teens are less Christian and more confused about moral and spiritual truth than ever."[28]

What's important to God, and by extension, what should be important to us? The Bible is full of value statements:

» Jesus came "full of truth and grace" (John 1:14).

» "Walk as children of light" (Ephesians 5:8).

» "The generous will be blessed" (Proverbs 22:9).

» "Be strong and courageous" (Joshua 1:9).

» "Speak the truth in love" (Ephesians 4:15).

» And putting God's mission above our own: "I must be about My Father's business" (Luke 2:49).

There are, of course, many others. A passage that is both endearing and challenging is in the apostle Paul's letter to the Colossians. He wrote,

> *Therefore, as God's chosen people, holy and dearly loved, clothe yourselves with compassion, kindness, humility, gentleness and patience. Bear with each other and forgive one another if any of you has a grievance against someone. Forgive as the Lord forgave you. And over all these virtues put on love, which binds them all together in perfect unity. Let the peace of Christ rule in your hearts, since as members of one body you were called to peace. And be thankful. Let the message of Christ dwell among you richly as you teach and admonish one another*

27 "Gen Z: Your Questions Answered," *Barna Group*, 6 Feb. 2018, https://www.barna.com/research/gen-z-questions-answered/.

28 Jonathan Morrow, "Only 4 Percent of Gen Z Have a Biblical Worldview," *Impact 360 Institute*, 26 May 2020, https://www.impact360institute.org/articles/4-percent-gen-z-biblical-worldview/.

> *with all wisdom through psalms, hymns, and songs from the Spirit, singing to God with gratitude in your hearts. And whatever you do, whether in word or deed, do it all in the name of the Lord Jesus, giving thanks to God the Father through him.* —Colossians 3:12-17 (NIV)

I'm not sure there's a better value statement in the Scriptures, but please, look for what's meaningful to you.

What difference does it make to live according to God's values? Christians in the first centuries after Christ were bright lights in the darkness of Roman culture. In the middle of two plagues in the second and third centuries, between one-quarter and one-third of the entire population died. Many pagans fled when one of their family members got sick, but Christians stepped in to care for them, even at the expense of their own lives. Their love and courage didn't go unnoticed. The percentage of believers in the Roman Empire rose from less than 1 percent to almost 50 percent! Compassion and courage, two fundamental values of God's kingdom, made a huge difference.

Lucian of Samosata was a pagan philosopher who despised the Christians. In *Passing of Peregrinus,* he mocked the believers of his day, but below the surface, we can see why the Christians had such a profound impact on the rest of the culture. Lucian wrote:

> *These deluded creatures, you see, have persuaded themselves that they are immortal and will live forever, which explains the contempt of death and willing self-sacrifice so common among them. It was impressed on them too by their lawgiver [Jesus] that from the moment they are converted, deny the gods of Greece, worship the crucified sage, and live after his laws, they are all brothers. They take his instructions completely on*

faith, with the result that they despise all worldly goods and hold them in common ownership.[29]

Is that how people outside the church think of you and me? Are they astounded that we're far more loyal to Jesus than to power, prestige, possessions, and popularity? Are they amazed at our generosity? Our compassion? Our confidence in a glorious future in heaven? If not, then we may need to work a little harder on our values—both to define them and to live by them.

In every age and in every culture, Christians are tempted to take the wrong gate, choose the wrong road, and bear inedible fruit. The foundations the world values look promising and attractive—after all, virtually everyone is counting on them! But God's beloved children have a far more secure foundation, a far better hope, and a far greater security in the grace of Jesus.

After Moses, Joshua took over to lead the people of Israel to take possession of the land God had promised to give them. He took them across the Jordan River and into the Promised Land, and there, they had to fight for the land God had given them. This tells us that even God's most precious promises often become a reality only through struggle. There is no promise of a care-free life when we follow Jesus, but there is the promise that when we're tested, God will deepen our faith, give us more wisdom, and shape our character.

At the end of the conquest of the land, Joshua gave a final benediction, but it wasn't just "Be blessed and be happy." It was a challenge to remind faithful to God no matter what:

So fear the Lord and serve him wholeheartedly. Put away forever the idols your ancestors worshiped when they lived beyond the Euphrates

29 Peter Kirby, "Lucian of Samosata," *Early Christian Writings* 2022, 10 Jan. 2022, <http://www.earlychristianwritings.com/lucian.html>.

> *River and in Egypt. Serve the Lord alone. But if you refuse to serve the Lord, then choose today whom you will serve. Would you prefer the gods your ancestors served beyond the Euphrates? Or will it be the gods of the Amorites in whose land you now live? But as for me and my family, we will serve the Lord.* —Joshua 24:14-15 (NLT)

When God's values become our values, they become guideposts to direct us and guardrails to protect us.

When God's values become our values, they become guideposts to direct us and guardrails to protect us. We may have to work hard to inject them into our own hearts, into our marriages, and into our relationships with our children, friends, and colleagues, but before long, they become the background music that reminds us that what we treasure really matters.

TIMING AND PERSISTENCE

It's not smart to wait until some future time to identify God's values and live by them. I sometimes hear singles say, "When I find the right person, we'll figure out what's important together." I want to say, "Really? Is that what you think happens?" Far too often, the person we hope will be magically transformed after the wedding does, in fact, change, but not in the positive direction! It's far, far better to craft strong, biblical values, so you become the right person instead of trying to find the right person.

There are three distinct times to focus on values: as early as possible, in the middle of relationships, and after a relational catastrophe. If we develop strong values early, they'll shape everything we think, say, and do for the rest of our lives. (In case you can't tell, I advocate that one!) But many of us coast in our relationships and careers until we're in the middle of a struggle, and we realize we need to determine what's really important and worthwhile. That's very common, and people are often highly motivated at that point. The third time is after a divorce, the death of a dream, a child has wandered off the path, death of a loved one, disease, or some other excruciating heartache. Pain certainly gets our attention, and it becomes a good tutor, but we pay a hefty price for waiting so long.

Let me get very specific and practical. I've seen families in which the teenage children have free rein to raise their voices and yell at their parents, especially their mother. Somehow, they picked up the idea that brutal honesty, no matter how much it hurts someone, is a family value. They may have seen one of their parents openly criticize the other, and they didn't see any repentance or resolution for the wound it caused. What do you think is going to happen when that teenager grows up and gets married? Yeah, it's inevitable.

But I've also seen parents step in to defend the spouse when a child is demanding or offensive. In my home, I've had to say on more than one occasion, "Don't talk to my wife that way! We value and honor people in our house, and we show respect even if we disagree about something."

Values are slippery. If we're not careful, they fall out of our hearts, our minds, our mouths, and our choices. We need to be persistent, and we need to be crystal clear. Let me offer a few recommendations:

1) Be a partner with your spouse (or if you're single, with a close friend) in identifying your family values. These conversations may challenge both of you (or maybe only one of you), but lean into these questions until you come to agreement.

2) Get input from people you admire, read a book on the subject, or talk to your friends or small group to get their input.
3) Make your values practical, portable, and emotional. I think five is a good number, but you may want as many as ten. Remember that fewer is better because they'll be easier to remember. Write them down, edit them so they're just right, and then post them somewhere so that everyone can see them. They need to be crisp, memorable, and specific. Vague values don't inspire anyone. If you can't tweet them, they're too long.
4) Be creative in how you talk about your stated values. Call them your "Family Mantra," "Playbook," "Users' Manual," "Creed," or something else. The point is that our values should inspire us, not depress or discourage us. If we communicate them and our kids roll their eyes, we may need to go back to the drawing board (unless, of course, the eye-rollers are teenagers, which is completely expected).
5) With your children, be sure to live your values, use object lessons to show them the effects of good and weak values, refer to passages of scripture, and reinforce them in countless ways. But the most important is to live them. If you do, you become the primary object lesson and model; if you don't, they'll conclude you're a hypocrite.
6) When you fail to live by your values (and you will, at least occasionally), be honest with people. Today, repentance is something we seldom talk about, but frequently repenting is a spiritual and relational 180, it's the way to stay close to the path God has set for you, and it shows that you're authentic, which is one of the primary values in any relationship.
7) As you become more committed to your values, you'll find ways to be sure every decision is sifted through this grid. There will

be adjustments and some hard conversations, but sooner or later (hopefully sooner) your values really will become the background music to everything that happens in your family.

This isn't busywork. This is one of the most important things you can do for yourself, your family, and all those who interact with you. For at least a month, go over your stated values every day with your spouse and children. Ask how they're making choices to live by them, and ask about their struggles to follow them. When they mess up, don't condemn. Instead, listen, affirm their honesty, and admit that learning to live by them is a process.

Gradually, the atmosphere of your home will change. You'll probably get some pushback from one or two people, but again, give them time and space. They're waiting to see if you're committed to live by them. When you prove yourself, they'll probably soften their resistance.

CLOSE THE GAP

How many people do you know who can clearly articulate their core beliefs and fundamental values? We all have values, but for most of us, they're just what others around us show that they think are important . . . and sadly those are seldom biblical values. The first step, then, is to realize that we need to invest some time in crafting our own. Then, as we take steps to live by them, we'll almost certainly expose the fact that we fall short of what we say is important.

For example, loving people just as Christ loves us? Well, let's don't talk about that one . . . or let's do. If that's a value I've identified, I need to dig deep to experience more of His love, so there's an overflow from my heart into the lives of others. No overflow, no love. And when I'm selfish, overly critical, passive, or less than loving, I need to confess it to God and experience His forgiveness, and then confess it to the person I've hurt and ask for that person's forgiveness. That's how we close the gap between what we say we value and how we live according to our values.

Not many of us reading this book are murderers, rapists, prostitutes, or thieves. The vast majority look good on the outside, but our internal values may still be rooted in what the world considers important: beauty, money, intelligence, status, and power. How can we tell? By how we respond when we get those things . . . and how we respond when our hopes for them are shattered. What do we think about when we have nothing pressing on our minds? Is it getting more stuff, having more fun, and rising to a position of more authority? Or is it gratitude for what we already have and the people who are around us and how we can represent Jesus to them even more?

Sooner or later, our values are tested, but few of us face a test as severe as my friend Sadia. She felt a strong call to serve her community as a police officer. After she graduated from the police academy, she began her career as a patrol officer. During the first two years of her new career, she met her future husband, Matthew, who also was a police officer. On the first night when they were partners, they received a "tone call," signifying an emergency. They sped to the scene with lights flashing and siren blaring. When they arrived, they found a man who had attempted suicide. After performing CPR, they were able to resuscitate him.

Intense situations like this built trust and admiration between Sadia and Matthew. Eventually, their relationship grew even deeper, and they got married. Later, when they looked back on their first emergency call together, they realized it had been a very unusual first date! They received a commendation from their department for their quick response and professionalism in handling the delicate, life-threatening situation.

Their marriage created a blended family. They later had two more daughters together. As a family with four girls, they found themselves juggling demands between work and home. Sadia eventually became a detective which allowed her to work days while Matthew worked the night shift as a patrol officer.

One night, Sadia was home watching a Disney movie with the girls when her phone rang. One of her friends asked if she was watching the news—a police officer had been shot. Her friend told her she needed to go to the scene. Sadia quickly got dressed, left the girls with her mother-in-law, and raced to the crime scene, which happened to be near a hospital.

On the way, she received a call from the police chief. Without revealing details, the chief told her to get to the scene as quickly as possible. Sadia immediately knew that Matthew was in danger. When she arrived at the scene, squad cars with flashing lights and media trucks had blocked the scene of the crime. She quickly saw that her worst nightmare had become a reality. Matthew and another officer had been shot, leaving Matthew dead and his partner seriously wounded. After several hours at the scene, Sadia went home at about 3:00 a.m., knowing that her life would never be the same.

In the days that followed, Sadia buried her beloved husband, began the process of grieving, and prepared to raise her daughters on her own. Through the pain, confusion, and mental fog, she took stock of her life, her values, her hopes, and her fears. She realized the fast-paced, dangerous career path she had chosen as a detective had collided with her calling as a mother. She had to make some hard but necessary decisions. She quit her job so she could spend more time with the girls.

As a single mother, Sadia had a choice. She could allow her circumstances to rob her of her hopes and dreams, or she could grow stronger through her struggles and challenges. She decided to go back to school to earn her credentials to teach. Today, she is teaching law enforcement at a local community college and using her story as a platform to encourage and inspire young police officers. The lesson she wants her students—and everyone she encounters, including her children—to understand is that we have no control over what happens to us.

Life can make us bitter or better. Rather than harboring anger toward the man who murdered Matthew or blaming God for taking away her husband and their girls' father, she chose to forgive, and she taught her daughters to forgive as well. She wants her girls to understand the importance of showing compassion toward others who face tragedies. She explains that we have no control over the things that life throws at us, but we can control how we respond.

Sadia has learned the importance of living out her values of forgiveness, faith, and perseverance. She is committed to the double win, imparting those values at home, and teaching them in her classes. Rather than being known as the lady who lost her husband and is living defeated and depressed, she has chosen to be known by her girls, her students, and to everyone she meets, as a woman who has learned to win by turning the most severe trial into a wonderful testimony.

BUILD THE HOUSE

We started this chapter by looking at Jesus' story of the two houses with different foundations. The problem wasn't the storm; the problem was in the construction. The storm just revealed that one house had a wise builder and the other a foolish one. In some parts of the country, the soil is made up largely of clay, which becomes a slimy mush when it rains and like concrete during dry spells. When people build houses on clay, they often have foundation problems which cause cracks in walls and floors. In those regions of the country, many companies offer their (expensive) services to dig under the houses and install concrete piers to stabilize the foundation.

You and your family are like a house. If it has cracks of resentment, anxiety, demands, and estrangement, it's time to call in the specialist to make repairs.

That's what I'm recommending to you. You and your family are like a house. If it has cracks of resentment, anxiety, demands, and estrangement, it's time to call in the specialist to make repairs. For yourself, your marriage, your family, or your team at the company:

- Find a wise person who will serve as the foundation specialist . . . not just anybody, but someone who has "been around the block" and has helped others find better values as a stronger foundation. This person may be an older friend, a pastor, or a counselor. Don't look for a quick conversation as the fix. It takes time and effort to dig underneath the house, install the new piers, level the foundation, and replace the dirt and plants.
- Make the investment. Stabilizing a cracked foundation costs a lot of money, it takes time, and it involves care to be sure it's right. Your

family is important to you, or you wouldn't be reading this book, so put your money and time where your heart is.

» Regularly check your foundation. Look for hairline cracks that may indicate it's time for an adjustment or two. We aren't machines; we're people with conflicting desires—and too often, wayward hearts. Let me use another metaphor: When airline pilots fly across the country, they (or their autopilots) make thousands of midcourse corrections to stay close to the flight plan. If you charted their actual flight, you'd see thousands of times they drifted off course. They make quick and minor corrections, so those of us on the planes don't even notice. If they waited too long, the passengers might find themselves in the wrong city, the wrong state, and maybe even the wrong country! Don't wait. Make those corrections!

THE VALUES QUESTION

What do you want to be known for?

→| Key principle: Significance is more important than success. |←

THINK ABOUT IT:

1) What are some reasons it's so easy to slip into self-effort instead of trusting God, and self-promotion instead of humility and gratitude?
2) As you think about passages of scripture that have been meaningful to you, what are the values that stand out to you?

3) When have you seen people (maybe including yourself) craft their values: from the beginning, in the middle of struggles, or after a calamity?
4) What are the benefits and liabilities of crafting them in each stage?
5) Why is it so important to live our values in front of our families, not just state them?
6) Take time to reflect (or continue to reflect) on these questions:

» What do I want to be known for?
» What's important in our marriage?
» What beliefs and lifestyle do I want to impart to my children (and grandchildren)?
» What influence do I want to have on the people around me (neighbors, friends, colleagues)?
» How can I live so that God will one day say to me, "Well done, good and faithful servant. Enter into the joy of your Master!"

Now, what are the values you're committed to live by? Talk about them, write them, and rewrite them until they're just right. Then post them in a conspicuous place where your family can see them every day.

CHAPTER 5

THE PRIORITIES QUESTION: WHAT'S (REALLY) IMPORTANT TO YOU?

The key is not to prioritize what's on your schedule,
but to schedule your priorities.
—Stephen Covey

Several years ago, Michelle and I wrote a book called *ReThink Life*. In the book, I tell the story of when we were visiting family in Texas. On the last night of our visit, we packed our bags, so we could leave early the next morning for our flight back to Orlando. I didn't sleep well that night because I anticipated the stress and strain of getting our kids up and dressed so we could get out the door by 4:30 a.m. to catch an early flight. In the early morning darkness, I got up, dressed, and started to load the car. To make as little noise as possible, I was barefoot. I started carrying several enormous suitcases down the winding staircase to the front door. In the pitch black darkness, I misjudged the last step where the surface changed from carpet to hardwood. I slipped, landed on my big toe, and sent suitcases flying through the air! I was in some serious pain. I probably broke my toe. (To this day, that toe doglegs to the right and hurts in cold weather.)

My mishap reminds me of what can happen when we misjudge the distance between what we say is important and our actual choices. It can create a lot of pain and frustration. When our choices don't match up with our good intentions, we make bad choices, and we spend a lot of time trying to remedy the disaster we've caused . . . or denying it even happened. No wonder we're so frustrated and stressed! Many of us are overcommitted. We've said "yes" to so much that we feel powerless to do the things we really want to do. Why do we keep doing this to ourselves? It's because we haven't recognized the difference between our intentions and our actual decisions.

Establishing our priorities is inextricably linked to our values: muddy values, slippery priorities; clear values, compelling priorities.

Establishing our priorities is inextricably linked to our values: muddy values, slippery priorities; clear values, compelling priorities. Even when we set priorities (think of New Year's resolutions), we seldom stick with them very long. We make a commitment to lose weight, so we buy a membership to a gym, but after a couple of weeks, our new workout clothes sit lonely in the drawer. In the business world, companies are well aware that what customers say they want may not be what they really want.

In an article in *Forbes*, Naomi Troni observes,

> *[There is an] apparent disconnect between intention and reality. We all know there's usually a gap between what consumers say and what they really do. After all, we're consumers, too, and we don't always live up to our aspirations of eating more healthfully, exercising more, flossing, or putting away money for a rainy day. Across most areas of life, people know what they "should" aspire to, but they struggle to put it into practice. For every Jamie Oliver [a health food chef] there are dozens of Paula Deens [give me that downhome cooking!].*[30]

We say our family relationships are really important, but we somehow find a way to go to one more meeting, take one more business trip, volunteer for one more activity, and be distracted by one more television show, email, or text.

We say saving and investing are important strategies for our future, but the latest smartphone looks so good, that vacation is so appealing, and that house or car will let us keep up with our friends.

We say we want to take care of our health, but the waffle fries at that fast-food restaurant are the best in town, we stay up because we don't want to miss the end of the movie, one bowl of ice cream won't hurt, and we can always start exercising next week.

---

30 Naomi Troni, "Marketing the Gap Between Intention and Action," *Forbes*, 17 Jul. 2012, https://www.forbes.com/sites/onmarketing/2012/07/17/marketing-the-gap-between-intention-and-action/?sh=2ef50a5b4ca9.

We say our relationship with God is the most important thing, but we go to church about once a month, our devotional reading and prayer are sporadic at best, and we're far more excited about people, events, recreation, and problems to fix than we are about knowing God.

We live in a culture that shouts, whispers, whines, and growls, "More!" And most of us don't want to be left behind. Comparison is the most common game in town. We keep an eye on what other people (especially our friends and colleagues) have, and we try like crazy to stay one step ahead of them . . . or at least even. What does this look like? Every product on the market has hundreds, if not thousands, of brands over a price range. If James and Susie got a new gadget for their house, I need one too. Which one shall I buy? The one that's $29.95 will probably work just fine, but the one James and Susie bought was $50. So, to keep from looking like I just stepped out of *The Walking Dead,* I buy the more expensive one!

How many decisions do we make to spend tiny, incremental amounts more than we really need to? Yeah, a lot! This is a classic relational-financial version of the frog in the kettle. Spending a little more just one time isn't a big deal, but hundreds of these choices every month have two detrimental effects: we spend more money than we wanted to, and we've let the decisions of others (I'm looking at you James and Susie!) run our lives.

Don't get me wrong. I'm not saying you should never upgrade, never spend a little more on a vacation, and never get the luxury package on a new car or truck, but I'm saying that you need to realize that the choices you're making may be coming from a place of insecurity and the desire to impress people. Think about it. You know it's true.

HARD BUT NECESSARY CHOICES

Matthew Emmons is an American marksman. In the 2004 Summer Olympic Games in Athens, Greece, Matthew was on his way to winning his second gold medal. In fact, he was so far ahead of the competition that all he had to do was hit the target anywhere, not even the bullseye, and the gold medal would be his. As Matthew looked at the target, he aimed high at 12 o'clock and slowly lowered the barrel of his gun—he took dead aim at the center of the target. He gently pulled the trigger and hit the bullseye. The crowd cheered, but suddenly Matthew realized he had a major problem. He aimed at the wrong target! He instantly moved from first to eighth place, losing the gold medal . . . and any medal. All of this happened because he was focused on the wrong target.

Have you ever confused activity with accomplishment? I know I have! Seminary professor and leadership expert Dr. Howard Hendricks observed, "The secret to concentration is elimination." In other words, we have to focus on less, so we can accomplish more. A Chinese proverb teaches, "If you chase two rabbits, both will escape." A divided focus always works against us! It causes us to major on the minors and minor on the majors. I love what Gary Keller, the founder of Keller Williams Realty, once said to an audience he was speaking to, "What's the one thing I can do, such that by doing it everything else is easier or unnecessary?"

Make sure your commitments reflect your priorities. When we know what's important "prior" to a decision, we can say "no" to the good, so we can say "yes" to the best. These are some of the most difficult choices in our lives, but they're absolutely necessary. You may have heard the story of the professor who brought to class a large bag of sand and a box of rocks. He asked a student to come to the front and told her to fill a large jar with sand. Then he told her, "Now, put the rocks in."

She shook her head and said, "There's no room."

He told her to dump the sand out on the table and fill the jar with rocks. When she was finished, he told her, "Now, is there room for sand?"

"Yes, some." She poured some sand into the jar until it was full.

The professor explained, "This is all about priorities. If we fill our lives with too many lesser priorities, we won't have time and space for the big, important things. Fill your schedule with big rocks first, then little rocks, and then, if there's any room left, with sand."

It's a simple but profound illustration. Are we prioritizing the big rocks of our relationship with God, our connection with those we love, our health, and our growth, or are our schedules consumed with the sand of conspicuous consumption, too many responsibilities, and endless pleasure? When we choose the most important things, a lot of others will be left out. Is this a choice you're willing to make for your heart, your marriage, your children, and your impact wherever you go? These choices show what's really important to us.

YOUR TOP FIVE

We are, as people have noted for generations, creatures of habit. Routines help us make sense of life, focus on what's important to us, and keep us on track. The problem, of course, is that many of us have developed habits that are (let me be kind) less than productive. We follow them, not because they're helpful, meaningful, and effective, but because they've become familiar—we don't stop to think about doing something different. In his book, *The Power of Habit*, Charles Duhigg observes:

> *Habits are powerful, but delicate. They can emerge outside our consciousness, or can be deliberately designed. Habits often occur without our permission, but can be reshaped by fiddling with their parts. They*

shape our lives far more than we realize—they are so strong, in fact, that they cause our brains to cling to them at the exclusion of all else, including common sense.[31]

We can't have good habits if we have too many commitments. Something has to give, and too often, it's by default, not by choice. Let me ask you a question: If you reduced your life to just five priorities that are most important to you, what would they be?

I can hear you now: "Five? Are you kidding?"

No, I'm not kidding. If we can have a laser focus on the few things that are most important (the big rocks), we'll have a far greater chance of succeeding in them. The keys are focus and consistency. That's where habits come in.

Many of us confuse activity with accomplishment, and the more frantic the activity, the more sure we are that we're on target. That's crazy . . . and crazy-making. We simply can't keep up this kind of pace all day every day, so we have to find some down time, even if it's not the best solution.

I know people who are consumed with responsibilities and hard decisions at work. They feel enormous pressure, either as owners or key employees. On the way home each day, they're still on the phone or texting to keep projects moving and solve problems. When they get home, they decompress. They're utterly spent emotionally, physically, and relationally. They sit in front of the television for hours, sometimes passive and sometimes irritable as their spouse and children clamor for their attention. But I also know people who experience such tension at home that their office (or their truck or their shop) is an escape for them. They can't be "all there" at work because they're preoccupied with the overwhelming drama at home.

---

31 Charles Duhigg, *The Power of Habit* (New York: Random House, 2014), 61.

One of the problems in modern life is that everything seems equally important. We have a hard time separating what's necessary from what's negotiable. That's why it's so instructive to wade into the exercise of identifying our top five priorities. We turn to the prophet Jeremiah again and listen as God speaks through him: "This is what the LORD says: 'Stop at the crossroads and look around. Ask for the old, godly way, and walk in it. Travel its path, and you will find rest for your souls'" (Jeremiah 6:16, NLT).

One of the problems in modern life is that everything seems equally important. We have a hard time separating what's necessary from what's negotiable.

When you identify what's most important, you'll undoubtedly circle back to the people and roles we've examined before, but this time, we'll be a bit more ruthless in saying "no" to anything that competes with these priorities. Let me offer some suggestions:

1. Your Faith

As we've seen, our relationship with God is the source of limitless love, joy, forgiveness, acceptance, wisdom, and strength. If there's not a sense of wonder that the God of Creation loves us enough to sacrifice Himself for us, we haven't yet grasped the concept of grace.

Our faith is rooted in the gospel. This message isn't just something that opens the door to meet God; it's our motivation to live for Him every day. The apostle Paul encouraged the Corinthians:

> *For Christ's love compels us, because we are convinced that one died for all, and therefore all died. And he died for all, that those who live should no longer live for themselves but for him who died for them and was raised again."* —2 Corinthians 5:14-15 (NIV)

Do you understand the wonder of grace more now than a year or two ago? Do you trust His wisdom more these days? Are you more patient, kind, and loving toward people who disagree with you? We love Him because He loved us first—and His love is richer, deeper, and more wonderful than we can imagine. Our love overflows into the lives of others—insiders and outsiders—because His love has overflowed into us.

Spiritual growth doesn't come naturally. We need to invest our time and our hearts to know God better and trust Him more. Who has God called you to be? The prophet Micah reminds us, "He has shown you, O mortal, what is good. And what does the Lord require of you? To act justly and to love mercy and to walk humbly with your God" (Micah 6:8, NIV). The proof of faith's reality is Monday's agenda.

The proof of faith's reality is Monday's agenda.

2. Your Most Important Relationships

Then, we look at the concentric circles of the people in our lives: our spouse and kids, then other members of our families, our closest friends, and other friends and colleagues. Experts who observe human connections say that the most accurate predictor of future happiness and fulfillment is the quality of our present relationships. King Solomon warned us: "Walk with the wise and become wise, for a companion of fools suffers harm" (Proverbs 13:20, NIV). But he also saw the positive side: "Two people are better off than one, for they can help each other succeed. If one person falls, the other can reach out and help. But someone who falls alone is in real trouble" (Ecclesiastes 4:9-10).

Loneliness was a real problem before the pandemic, and it has become deeper and more widespread with all of the lockdowns, masks, and a pervasive fear of getting too close to people. Ali Cashin described the findings of a Harvard study:

> *. . . 36% of all Americans—including 61% of young adults and 51% of mothers with young children—feel "serious loneliness." Not surprisingly, loneliness appears to have increased substantially since the outbreak of the global pandemic.*
>
> *The report also explores the many types of loneliness, various causes of loneliness, and the potentially steep costs of loneliness, including early mortality and a wide array of serious physical and emotional problems, including depression, anxiety, heart disease, substance abuse, and domestic abuse. While Americans clearly need to adopt distancing measures to curb the spread of the novel coronavirus, the report authors argue that we also must take steps to alleviate loneliness, particularly for the populations the survey suggests are most affected.*[32]

How do we alleviate loneliness? By moving toward each other, taking time to understand each other, and showing compassion for each other.

---

32 Ali Cashin, "Loneliness in America: How the Pandemic Has Deepened an Epidemic of Loneliness," *Making Caring Common*, 13 Dec. 2021, https://mcc.gse.harvard.edu/reports/loneliness-in-america.

When we're too busy, too preoccupied, too self-absorbed to connect with the most important people in our lives, so they feel deeply known and loved, something needs to change. We may have a lot of responsibilities, but love comes first. The apostle Paul wrote, "Above all, clothe yourselves with love, which binds us all together in perfect harmony" (Colossians 3:14, NLT).

Each of us has a built-in longing to be both fully known and deeply loved. Expressions of love without a deep grasp of what's important to the other person comes across as superficial, but when someone knows a lot about us but isn't loving, it's terrifying! Strong, enduring, life-transforming relationships are based on the twin pillars of understanding and love.

Is love really that important? Can't we assume that all of our activity is a demonstration of love for our spouse and kids? No, not really. Many years ago, B. B. Warfield studied the emotions of Jesus that are described in the Gospels. He found that one emotion was mentioned more than all the others combined: compassion. It means to be moved to the depths in our love, empathy, and care for another person. In many of the accounts in the four gospels, Jesus stopped what He was doing to give focused attention to the person in front of Him. Was He busy? Well, His mission was rescuing the world from sin and death. That's a pretty tall order! But He wasn't too busy to be moved so deeply that He stopped to show how much He cared.[33] We say we want to "follow Jesus." That means many things, but certainly, it means slowing down enough to be moved in the depths of our hearts to focus our attention—and our love—on the people around us.

---

33 B. B. Warfield, "The Emotional Life of Our Lord," *Biblical and Theological Studies by Members of the Faculty of Princeton Theological Seminary* (New York: Charles Scribner's Sons, 1912).

Be practical and gracious in how you recreate the family culture around this kind of love. Learn to ask great questions—without coming across as a prosecutor! And develop the skills of active listening. Instead of thinking about the next thing you want to say while another person is talking, wade in and ask a second and third question to understand more fully. Mirror the person's feelings, so he or she knows you get it, and occasionally say something like this: "Here's what I hear you saying. . . ."

Couples, make regular date nights. Dads, have dates with your daughters, and moms, with your sons. Have a rule that there will be no devices during meals . . . and by all means, plan at least three dinners together every week. (Yes, I know, you're too busy. But that's exactly the point: you're too busy!) Have game nights, camping trips, and visits to places where you form unforgettable moments and memories. Find out what's important to the people you love and make time for those activities.

3. Your Values

I want to circle back to this, not because I can't remember what I wrote earlier but because it's so important. I recommended that you settle on a few values. If you haven't done that already, it's time. Here are two suggestions:

» Think about your eightieth birthday party. What do you want your kids, grandkids, and great-grandkids to say about you? What are the kinds of stories you hope they'll tell? What is the look on their faces as they tell them? That day may seem impossibly far off (especially if you're the parent of infants or toddlers!), but it's a really good guide to determine what you need to do today to have that kind of response in the future.

» Conduct a "30 Days to Live" test. If your doctor told you that you only have thirty days to live, what would you stop doing, and what would you make sure you did? This is a wonderful question to ask in a family discussion.

4. Your Calling

Some Christians assume that if they're not pastors or missionaries, they don't have a true calling. Let me disabuse you of that idea! Our primary calling isn't to a role, but to a Person. We've been chosen, adopted, forgiven, and placed by our wise and sovereign God. He has equipped us to represent Him in everything we do, everywhere we go, and with everyone who crosses our path. There are no second-class Christians. The apostle Paul was with the Ephesians for three years, but when he wrote to them when he was in prison in Rome, he wanted to remind them, "For we are God's masterpiece. He has created us anew in Christ Jesus, so we can do the good things he planned for us long ago" (Ephesians 2:10).

Your careers are what you get paid for, but your calling is what you were made for.

Your careers are what you get paid for, but your calling is what you were made for. When you get up each day, you're on a mission. Whatever is on your business card, or if you don't have a business card, God has called you to be His partner in rescuing the lost, making disciples, and changing the world—nothing less than that! The problem, of course, is that many believers have the wrong assumption that their pastors and church staff members are paid to have that kind of impact, and their role is to give some money, so this work can be done. God wants much more than our money. He wants our hearts, our passion, our devotion, our words, and our courage to step into the darkness around us to represent Jesus.

The apostle Peter's letters were written to people outside Jerusalem decades after the resurrection. By this time, many Gentiles had believed, but Christians were being persecuted for their faith. He encouraged them, "You are a chosen people. You are royal priests, a holy nation, God's very own possession. As a result, you can show others the goodness of God, for he called you out of the darkness into his wonderful light" (1 Peter 2:9-10, NLT). The term "God's very own possession" is taken from Exodus 19. The term means "treasure." God considers you to be His treasure. He delights in you! Who doesn't want to tell others about a love like that!

5. Your Growth

Many people focus on self-fulfillment instead of self-development. Fulfillment, I've found, is a natural consequence of growing in every way, but we need a plan. Business owners don't just hope their companies will grow; they create a specific plan. Gardeners don't assume their flowers will bloom; they find out what kind of fertilizer to use, how much to water, and where to plant them. Athletes don't roll out of bed and expect to be champions; they practice, work out, listen to coaches, eat well to energize their bodies, and practice even more.

People who don't have a growth plan usually don't grow much. They coast, or they ricochet from one activity to another. I recommend charting a workable, effective plan to "fertilize" your heart, prioritize your relationships, stretch your mind, and make you physically stronger. And like a business owner, a gardener, or an athlete, be both persistent and patient. Substantive change takes time.

John Maxwell recommends that people spend 70 percent of their time and energy using their strengths. Do what you do best. Run your race, not someone else's. And if you insist on multitasking, you're probably diluting your focus on your strengths. It's a good idea to invest 25 percent of your time and energy in learning new concepts and skills, which leaves you the remaining 5 percent to improve your weaknesses.[34] That's a growth plan that works!

ROADBLOCKS AND DEAD ENDS

So, what are the reasons we aren't successful in our top five priorities? There may be a million reasons, but we'll focus on another top five:

1. A Misplaced Why

As pastor Andy Stanley famously stated, "Vision leaks."[35] If we don't pay attention, we'll certainly drift off course. That's why many companies post their mission and vision statements where employees can see them, and the executives (at least the smart ones) connect current initiatives and products to their overarching corporate purpose. How often do we need to be reminded why we do what we do? As often as it takes, especially in times of transition or trouble.

---

34 John Maxwell, *The 21 Indispensable Qualities of a Leader* (San Francisco: HarperCollins, 2007), p. 54.

35 Andy Stanley, "Vision Leaks," *Leadership*, Winter 2004, pp. 68-72.

2. Distractions

It doesn't take much, does it? We can become preoccupied with almost anything: the latest gadget, a dispute with a friend, financial strains, the stock market, planning for a vacation, daydreaming about winning the lottery, traffic, or something someone said that hurt our feelings, to name only a few. Some of these things demand our focused attention, so we can resolve them and get back to what matters most, but others are sideshows that occupy too much space in our heads for far too long.

3. Trouble

We're a "double exposure": we live in the tension between "the already" and the "not yet." We're miraculously saved, but the effects of the fall caused by sin are still with us and in us, and in case you haven't noticed, we live in a fallen world. Jesus promised we'd suffer tribulations, and that promise is fulfilled day after day! We face challenges at work, at home, in our health, with aging parents, teenage angst, and countless other struggles. We'll handle them better when we learn to see them as tests God wants to use to strengthen us.

When we think God has promised us an easy life, or that He'll give us relief from pain quickly and completely, it shows that we haven't read much from the Bible! Every person who walked with God suffered. Two that come to mind are Job and Jesus. Both of them lived righteous lives but experienced enormous suffering. The apostle Paul, too, experienced a wide range of troubles, from unjust criticism to being whipped and stoned. At one point, he had a "thorn in the flesh." We don't know what it was, but it bothered him a lot. He explained how he coped:

> *Three different times I begged the Lord to take it away. Each time he said, "My grace is all you need. My power works best in weakness." So now I*

am glad to boast about my weaknesses, so that the power of Christ can work through me. That's why I take pleasure in my weaknesses, and in the insults, hardships, persecutions, and troubles that I suffer for Christ. For when I am weak, then I am strong. —2 Corinthians 12:8-10 (NLT)

4. Opposition

Sometimes, the trouble comes from people, not just difficult circumstances. They may just annoy us, they may physically threaten us, or they may occupy someplace in between. People can hurt us in all kinds of ways, to all degrees, for any length of time. Today, the default position when there's any disagreement is to demonize the other person. That's not how Jesus responded to unfair criticism! He loved even the religious leaders who conspired to murder Him.

We need to remember that the best way to love those who are acting in unlovely ways is to treat them with a powerful combination of truth and grace. It's not loving to let addicts, liars, irresponsible people, and abusers keep going down their dark paths. Jesus stepped into the lives of outcasts to assure them of His forgiveness and His power to change lives, and He confronted the religious leaders, but not to bludgeon them. He was offering them a different path of grace. When we speak the truth with love to people who oppose us, we may win a few, but we need to be realistic that some won't join us on the path of honesty and reconciliation. Love them anyway. Pray for them, keep speaking truth to them until they say they don't want to hear it any longer, and never stop praying for them.

5. Fear

Some of us are very much aware of our anxiety. We feel threatened, and it doesn't take much to stop us from pursuing genuine change.

Others, though, suffer the debilitating effects of fear, but it has become so normal that they don't even notice it any longer. Change requires courage and sacrifice. If it were easy, everyone would do it! We don't draw on our own resources; we draw on the wisdom and power of the Holy Spirit to equip us, lead us, and transform us from the inside out. From hints in the apostle Paul's letters to his protégé, Timothy, we can assume that Timothy wrestled with self-doubt. Paul encouraged him, "For God has not given us a spirit of fear and timidity, but of power, love, and self-discipline" (2 Timothy 1:7, NIV).

John C. Maxwell has written, "Everything worthwhile in life—everything you want, everything you desire to achieve, everything you want to receive—is uphill," and he explained, "We have uphill hopes but downhill habits."[36] In this chapter, we've revisited some of the concepts found earlier in the book, but here, we've focused on developing new, healthy habits that make these priorities a normal part of our lives.

THE PRIORITIES QUESTION:

What's (really) important to you?

→| Key principle: Say "no" to the good, so you can say "yes" to the best. |←

36 John Maxwell, *No Limits*, also "The View from the Top of the Hill," July 12, 2016, https://www.johnmaxwell.com/blog/the-view-from-the-top-of-the-hill/.

THINK ABOUT IT:

1) On a scale of 0 (not on the radar) to 10 (off the charts), how would you rate your current success and fulfillment in each of these areas? Explain your rating for each one.

   ______Your faith

   ______Your most important relationships

   ______Your values

   ______Your calling

   ______Your growth

2) Take some time to plan for one step you want to take in each of these areas.
3) Now, look at the other areas. Create a workable, effective plan to "fertilize" your heart, prioritize your relationships, stretch your mind, and make you physically stronger. What do you need to say "no" to, so you can say "yes" to what's most important?
4) Which of the five "roadblocks and dead ends" have you experienced in the past few years? How did you respond?
5) Which ones are you experiencing now? What difference does it (or will it) make to see these as tests to help you grow wiser and stronger?

CHAPTER 6

THE EXPECTATIONS QUESTION: WHO DOES WHAT BY WHEN?

Three things you control every day are your attitude, your effort, and your actions to be a great teammate.

—Jon Gordon

It was a classic example of a longshot. In the depths of the Depression, nine young men were desperate to get college degrees, but they came from families that couldn't afford tuition, books, and housing. They had to earn scholarships if there were any chance to make it. One of those guys was Joe Rantz, a rawboned, tough kid whose parents couldn't afford to feed him—and in fact, didn't even want him around—so when he was in high school, he moved into an abandoned house at a logging camp to earn enough money to eat. He wanted to escape his abject poverty, so he tried out for the rowing team at the University of Washington. Rantz and the other eight are immortalized in Daniel James Brown's bestseller, *The Boys in the Boat*. The men practiced incessantly, trying to perfect their coordination and rhythm. They won races over perennial powers like Cal-Berkeley, and amazingly, they won the national championship against crews on the East Coast that were far more highly regarded. The win was a ticket to the Olympics in Berlin. The 1936 Games were designed by Adolph Hitler to showcase the supremacy of the Aryan race. Germany built large and lavish venues for the games, including rowing. In the finals, the Americans were assigned to the worst lane, but they used all of their training to synchronize their oars to the call of the coxswain and sprint to the finish line. Amazingly, these nine boys from poor backgrounds beat the finest teams in the world. They became Olympic champions!

I love this story because the teamwork required in rowing competitions fascinates me. They face the rear and listen to the (always short and light) coxswain call out the beat of the oars. The alignment, synchrony, and precision of all eight blades flawlessly hitting the water at exactly the same time is impressive, and the speed they generate is awe inspiring. It's the perfect example of the acronym T.E.A.M. (Together Everyone Achieves More). Imagine if we could get that same alignment, teamwork, and synergy in our marriages, with our children, in our friendships, and at work.

Unfortunately, the lofty expectations of the wedding day can turn sour when those expectations aren't met . . . and quite often, it doesn't take long. When little disagreements (or in rowing terms, "catching a crab" with the oar) aren't addressed and resolved, they can become big issues that divide and derail marriages. We're not talking about huge, life-changing issues. We can disagree over how to load the dishwasher, how and when to clean the bathrooms, who cooks and who cleans up, where dirty clothes go, relating to in-laws, handling money, sexual appetites, and plenty of other topics. And when we add children to the mix, we can have conflict over cell phones, homework, sports, chores, bedtime, the choice of friends, and on and on and on.

Every single interaction—that's how often expectations come into play in our relationships at home and at work. Our frustration level is based on the difference between our expectations and reality. Who's to blame? Almost always, it takes two (at least!).

Our frustration level is based on the difference between our expectations and reality. Who's to blame? Almost always, it takes two (at least!).

The signs of unfulfilled expectations are found in the litany of the ways strains show up in our most important connections. We're quick to assign blame—some are "blame throwers" and some are "blame sponges," and these two always seem to find each other. We may blow up and shout, trying to intimidate the other person into compliance, or we may use passive-aggressive tactics, looking innocent but inflicting pain on the other person. We may use silence to punish, or we may run away to escape the frustration. If someone asks, "What's wrong?" we may shrug and say, "Nothing," when that's obviously not true, or we may bring out a catalog of offenses (real or imagined) inflicted on us. All in all, we're very creative in ways we mishandle unfulfilled expectations!

ASSUMED OR ARTICULATED?

"He should know better!" I've heard that statement come from the mouths of plenty of women, but I've heard similar moans from men. "Shoulds" seldom produce understanding and cooperation. We often assume a spouse, child, friend, or colleague should read our minds and know what makes us happy or sets us off. In my conversations with couples, expecting a spouse to read minds has never proven to be a workable strategy.

It's important to articulate expectations, and when (not if) there's disagreement, negotiate a compromise. I know couples who have gone for days without speaking because the husband rearranged the dishes before starting the dishwasher. His wife was furious that he didn't value her efforts, and she took it very personally. He was equally resentful that she didn't appreciate that his placement of dishes and glasses was more precise and reduced the chance of anything being chipped. Do you think that's a ridiculous example? I've got plenty more I could tell you about, including the choice of restaurants, the temperature of the house, buying furniture, laundry habits, and what to do on vacations.

Articulating our expectations is much more than stating our list of demands. That may be a starting point, but it's not a very good one. Let me offer some questions to ask ourselves during a time of low tension in the relationship:

» Do I insist that my way is the right way . . . the only right way?

For many of us, being right is the ultimate validation, and it's so vital that we can't let it go. I've heard a wife or husband complain, "You always have to be right!" That's a problem that goes to the heart of the person's sense of identity and security, and it creates deep resentment in others.

» Do I value differences?

Without a foundational appreciation for the other person's strengths, points of view, and values, virtually every interaction turns into a short fuse on a big bomb.

» Is "compromise" a dirty word?

Some people think so. They refuse to give an inch "out of principle." But actually, it's out of pride or the fear of showing any weakness or losing control.

» Do I really try to understand my spouse's perspective, hopes, and desires?

We need to enter into conversations so deeply that we can articulate our spouse's love and longing as well as he or she can. That's a very high bar, and a necessary one.

» What message am I communicating to our children?

In case you didn't realize it, they're watching every facial expression, listening to every word, and internalizing every emotion you display. There are many reasons to do some hard work to change and articulate expectations, and this is a big one.

In my opinion, one of the most important roles of spouses is to create an atmosphere that brings out the very best in each person—like the boys in the boat. It takes teamwork to make the dream work, and each person's contribution is vital. All of us have strengths and areas that need some improvement. Instead of despising each other for falling short in some way, we need to go farther to encourage, support, and affirm people, especially when they've messed up. Unrealistic expectations inevitably lead to conflict, but the tension may simmer under the surface for weeks, months, or even years. When this happens, pride, demands, jealousy, selfishness, and stubbornness sabotage relationships and create a toxic environment. Do you think that assessment is too harsh? Come sit with me as I talk to couples.

Unrealistic expectations inevitably lead to conflict, but the tension may simmer under the surface for weeks, months, or even years. When this happens, pride, demands, jealousy, selfishness, and stubbornness sabotage relationships and create a toxic environment.

The same principles apply in all our relationships. Unrealistic expectations create tension, division, and heartache in friendships, with our neighbors, and at work. Can anything be done about it? Yes, stay tuned.

PICK ME!

It would be very easy to focus on our spouse's problems with expectations (or a child, adult child, friend, or colleague), but let's shine the spotlight on ourselves. We need to own our part in the equation. In other words, change begins with you and me.

We can fail in two main ways: by not measuring up to reasonable expectations of others or by demanding that someone meet our exceptionally high standards. Either way, we're the ones who need to make some adjustments. When we fail in either of these ways . . .

» Respect takes a hit.

Our behavior may work like sandpaper to gradually erode trust as we use relatively small but persistent criticisms to make our point, or an outburst of rage may shatter trust, even if we promise it won't happen again.

» Distance grows.

We can live under the same roof and sleep in the same bed, but when we fail in either of these ways, we get more than a cold shoulder. Without rectifying the problem, suspicion and isolation become the new norm.

» Anger turns into resentment.

Anger is the number one tool our spiritual enemy uses to sabotage relationships. He knows if he can get us angry and keep us angry, he'll defeat us. There's nothing wrong with the feeling of anger when it's directed toward injustice, but if it's not resolved, it soon transforms into bitterness, resentment, and contempt. For many couples, this sooner or later approaches a point of no return, or at least that's what they conclude. That's why we must keep honor high and anger low.

» Molehills become mountains.

You know exactly what I'm talking about. We may have overlooked a quirk before, or we may even have thought it was cute, but now, things are very different. Making that funny noise when he's chewing, taking so long to get ready, forgetting the keys . . . almost anything can be a spark that ignites the spilled gasoline of suspicion and resentment.

Where do our expectations come from? What has shaped them into what they are today? Undoubtedly, there are a number of factors, but a few are probably most important. First, your childhood and your experiences in your home. Children soak up the atmosphere of their home life, for good, for ill, or almost always, in between. The spectrum of family life is incredibly broad, from loving, stable, supportive parents and siblings to severe abuse and abandonment. We may have grown up with a parent who is an alcoholic or addict, with a mentally or physically challenged sibling, in poverty or wealth, with a parent in the military who came back with PTSD, enduring frequent moves to new cities and new friends, or any of a myriad of other ways security was undermined. Even in the best of homes, when we were teenagers, most of us thought our parents were dumb, but by the time we had our own children, we began to see how wise they were when we were with them every day.

Second, our culture had an impact on our expectations. Our peer group when we were adolescents shaped us, the music we listened to, the movies we watched, and the television shows we enjoyed (and still enjoy) cultivate particular expectations of the way life and relationships ought to be. And our present peer group continues to shape us.

And third, comparison is a powerful factor in shaping our sense of identity. It's human nature to check out where we are on several pecking orders: our intelligence, beauty, wealth, athleticism, and the ever important "cool factor." Comparison may be normal, but in people who assume they're in the back of the pack, it creates enormous insecurity. Actually, except for the smartest, most handsome or beautiful, rich, athletic, and cool people on the planet, all of us come up short. Our insecurity makes us emotionally and psychologically fragile, easily hurt, and longing for approval. We hope (expect, demand) that people come through for us with exquisite compassion, praise, and appreciation. (How well does that work out for us?)

THE WAY BACK, THE WAY FORWARD

Some of us need to do some remedial work to restore trust and begin to create harmony and teamwork, but since respect is fragile and can easily be eroded, all of us need to practice important relationship principles:

1) Value the team.

   A big part of premarital counseling is helping men and women see the "we" more than just the "I." As the relationship continues in the early years, and then if they have children, the pressures grow, so it's easier to avoid good communication. Assumptions lead to misunderstandings, and demands crush compromise. As a practical step, make a list of the family values that are important to both of you. You might have two lists: "What's important to us?" and "Who do we want to become as a family?" These brief documents become the launchpad for many meaningful discussions and a framework for resolving conflict.

2) Develop negotiating skills.

   A study by Harvard Law School found that when both parties are satisfied with a negotiation, they are more likely to uphold the terms of the deal. And if both parties are happy, they'll probably be willing to negotiate the next time, and the next.[37] One of the most important steps in negotiating is to agree on the process: "This is the way we'll talk about this," "This is a win for both of us," "This is how we'll handle disagreements." If the process is agreed to, the two people have a much better chance of coming to a positive solution. Another crucial skill is mirroring, that is, reflecting back what the other person is communicating. We can say, "This is what

37 "Managing Expectations in Negotiations," *Harvard Law School*, 8 Nov. 2021, https://www.pon.harvard.edu/daily/conflict-resolution/managing-expectations/.

I hear you saying." If we're right, the other person feels understood. If we're off base, the person can say, "That's not quite it. Let me explain it again."

3) Practice confession and repentance.

   Some faith traditions include confession and assurance of forgiveness in every worship service, but for some of us, it's not emphasized as often. When Martin Luther nailed the "95 Theses" to the cathedral door at Wittenberg, the first one read, "When our Lord and Master Jesus Christ said, 'Repent' (Mt. 4:17), he willed the entire life of believers to be one of repentance."[38] In other words, confession and repentance need to be as regular and normal for us as breathing! Confession is owning our part in any problem: "I was wrong. Please forgive me." Repentance is the commitment to change our words, our attitude, and our behavior: "Here's what I want to do next time. I can do better. I will do better." Decades ago, one of the characters in the movie *Love Story* famously said, "Love means never having to say you're sorry." That may sound noble and sweet on the big screen, but it doesn't work in real life. Love means saying you're sorry as often as you misunderstand, hurt, ignore, intimidate, run from, or demand compliance from someone you love.

4) Become more comfortable with disagreement.

   When someone responds to a problem with disproportionate displays of emotion, it's a sure indicator that something is broken under the hood. It's one thing to say, "I'll value what you say even if I disagree," but radical insecurity often overrides this commitment. When we're easily threatened, even by the slightest thing, we react

38 Martin Luther, "The 95 Theses," https://www.luther.de/en/95thesen.html.

defensively or offensively instead of entering into a conversation to understand, negotiate, and resolve the issue. A simple disagreement doesn't have to start World War III!

We're creatures of habit—we react the same way to the same things over and over again. To change and create new, healthy habits, we need to invest our hearts and minds in new responses. Experts say that new habits are established in thirty days if people stick to it. It would be a magnificent gift to the person you love to commit to a month of honest conversation, valuing differences, and negotiating agreements on everything that bothers one or both of you.

We're creatures of habit—we react the same way to the same things over and over again. To change and create new, healthy habits, we need to invest our hearts and minds in new responses.

The latter part of most of the apostle Paul's letters are filled with practical instructions. He explains the wonder of God's amazing grace in the first chapters, and he makes applications in the last ones. For instance, in Romans 12, Paul explains how our experience of the unconditional love of God should shape our most significant relationships:

Don't just pretend to love others. Really love them. Hate what is wrong. Hold tightly to what is good. Love each other with genuine affection, and take delight in honoring each other. Never be lazy, but work hard and serve the Lord enthusiastically. Rejoice in our confident hope. Be patient in trouble, and keep on praying. When God's people are in need, be ready to help them. Always be eager to practice hospitality.

Bless those who persecute you. Don't curse them; pray that God will bless them. Be happy with those who are happy, and weep with those who weep. Live in harmony with each other. Don't be too proud to enjoy the company of ordinary people. And don't think you know it all! —Romans 12:9-16 (NLT)

In this passage, we find the keys to teamwork in a family (and everywhere else we go). When we love with genuine affection and delight in honoring each other, we lower our guard and we eliminate the other person's reason to be defensive. Kindness, generosity, and compassion break down barriers—even in relationships that have been little more than an armed truce for years. And Paul ends this section with a call to humility: "Don't think you know it all!" Isn't that at the heart of our misguided expectations? Isn't humility the key to slowing down long enough to really listen, to valuing the other person's opinion, and finding common ground, so we live in harmony?

Sure it is.

THE COURAGE TO CHANGE

Let me share a couple of stories to show how people have implemented the concepts in this chapter.

I had the privilege of participating in the ribbon-cutting ceremony of a local business. It was exciting—scores of people stood in line for the grand opening of The Naked Cupcake. It's always exciting when a new business opens, especially one that spreads joy to so many people. Who doesn't love cupcakes? What most people don't see are the sacrifices, long hours, disappointments, and setbacks in starting a business. The headaches that come with starting a business can also take its toll on a marriage and family.

For years, Sandra was a school teacher. She loved spreading joy to children. However, one day she started feeling that her calling to be a teacher was coming to end. She had always dreamed of starting her own business baking cupcakes. She remembered cooking as a little girl, and her passion for cupcakes began to grow when she saw the joy on other people's faces when they were eating cupcakes. Sandra decided to transition from being a teacher to start a cupcake business. However, for that to work, she and her husband, Nick, were going to have to trade off on their roles at home and in the business.

They started their business as a food truck to serve parties and events. As the business grew, they realized their need to have a permanent store of their own to serve more joy to their customers. They quickly learned having a permanent, storefront location was going to be harder than they thought. It was going to require a lot more time on Sandra's part, a significant financial investment, and heightened risks during a pandemic. After two years of laying the groundwork for the launch of their new store, their vision finally became a reality. I asked Nick, "How did you do it with two small children?"

He answered, "I never dreamed my role would be the primary caretaker for our children, but I quickly realized it was the role I needed to play during this season to free my wife up to do what only she could do. She needed to invest her time in being trained, understanding and implementing the business plan, and recruiting the right team of people to make the dream a reality." He continued, "We're committed to each other and our kids. We're a team, and we're in this together. We work hard to serve each other however and wherever we can. We know we can accomplish something great together when we play to each other's strengths and are willing to serve and support each other in the process. It's the only way we can win at work and home—when both places are calling our names at the same time."

Our friends Jacob and Syd Charisse have a remarkable story that defies the odds for having a thriving marriage and family along with thriving careers. They met when they were both on the track team at the University of Missouri. After graduating from college, Jacob got a job in Wisconsin, while Syd Charisse stayed in Missouri to pursue medical school. Even though the distance created difficulties, they decided to get married.

Jacob commuted for nine months until a door opened for Syd Charisse to transfer to a medical school where Jacob was living. This allowed them to finally be together. They had their first child when Syd Charisse started her residency program, six years after they were married. At this time, they were both working 80 to 100 hour weeks with a new baby. They knew it was going to require a lot of flexibility and sacrifice to make it work. People warned them that being in the medical profession and staying married was going to be difficult because of the long hours and demands. Knowing this, Jacob made a commitment to eat every meal in the break room with Syd Charisse, even if she may have only fifteen minutes or thirty minutes before being paged. That was their way of being together making the most of their situation.

After Syd Charisse finished her residency, she decided to work part-time at a local urgent care facility and part-time at the ER. This allowed Jacob to advance in his career, and it allowed them to have more children. Eventually, they had four beautiful children. Syd Charisse was honored to serve as one of the doctors for the World Games in Athens,

Greece, for the US Track and Field Team, and she has continued to thrive in her medical career. Jacob became the CEO of a company that supplies energy to multiple states in the Southeast.

Fast-forward: They've been married for over thirty years, defying all the odds as an interracial couple. When I asked how they learned how to win at work and win at home, their answers sound very strange to some people, but their strategy has proven to be the secret to their success. They put their relationship with God and each other before anything else. Couples are often tempted to put their marriage on the back burner when children enter the picture, and the children take center stage. However, Syd Charisse and Jacob put their marriage first, and they made sure their children understood their priorities.

They went on date nights every week. They supported each other through different seasons in their careers and with their growing family. They divided and conquered to make it all work, from Jacob doing laundry and the dishes to Syd Charisse driving the kids to school and other activities. They never sacrificed their marriage or family life on the altar of endless demands or opportunities. Even when their kids became involved in extracurricular activities and sports, Jacob volunteered to manage the scheduling for practices and games. He intentionally scheduled games, so they didn't interfere with church.

To protect and prioritize their marriage and family, they set boundaries at work by never meeting alone with someone of the opposite sex. They were in constant communication with each other about any surprises in their schedules or awkward work-related meetings with someone of the opposite sex. They never allowed work, travel schedules, friendships, or their kids' sports to come before their marriage—and everyone around them knew it. They had seen too many couples prioritize their careers or their children and suffer the consequences. Being their best at home allowed them to be their best at work and has allowed their family to thrive during all these years.

Winning at home and work is possible, but it requires courage and a commitment to put your marriage first no matter what. When couples repeat their wedding vows, ". . . for better or for worse, through sickness and in health, for richer or for poorer," those are the parts of the relationship where couples must learn to pivot, make necessary changes, and support each other, so everyone in the family can thrive and reach their full potential.

If you're a single parent, the weight of these roles and responsibilities are single-handedly being carried on your shoulders. No one understands the load you carry more than you. You can win at home and at work if you take care of yourself, so you remain physically, spiritually, and emotionally healthy for your kids. It's why the flight attendants tell parents to put the oxygen masks on themselves first before putting it on their children during an emergency. What's the purpose? So the parent is able to stay strong and alert to be able to carry out the other necessary requirements to ensure their child's safety and well-being.

Humility, courage, and wisdom. These are the valuable and necessary traits for those who combine dreams with rigorous honesty.

Humility, courage, and wisdom. These are the valuable and necessary traits for those who combine dreams with rigorous honesty. That's how we set, communicate, and fulfill our expectations to one another.

THE EXPECTATIONS QUESTION:

Who does what by when?

→| Key principle: It takes teamwork to make the dream work. |←

THINK ABOUT IT:

1) Think of the last interpersonal tension you experienced. What was the difference between your expectation (or someone's expectation of you) and reality?
2) What are some of the painful consequences that happen when we fail to meet another person's expectations . . . and when they fail to meet ours?
3) How do you think your childhood experiences shaped your expectations and reactions in disagreements?
4) What specific negotiating skills do you need to develop? What difference will it (or they) make?
5) Take some time to discuss these topics with your spouse, or if you're single, with a close friend: "What's important to us/me?" and "Who do we want to become as a family?"

6) What's the power of confession and repentance in a relationship? Does owning your part in a strained relationship terrify you, make you angry, or inspire you? Explain your answer.

PART 3

REENGAGE

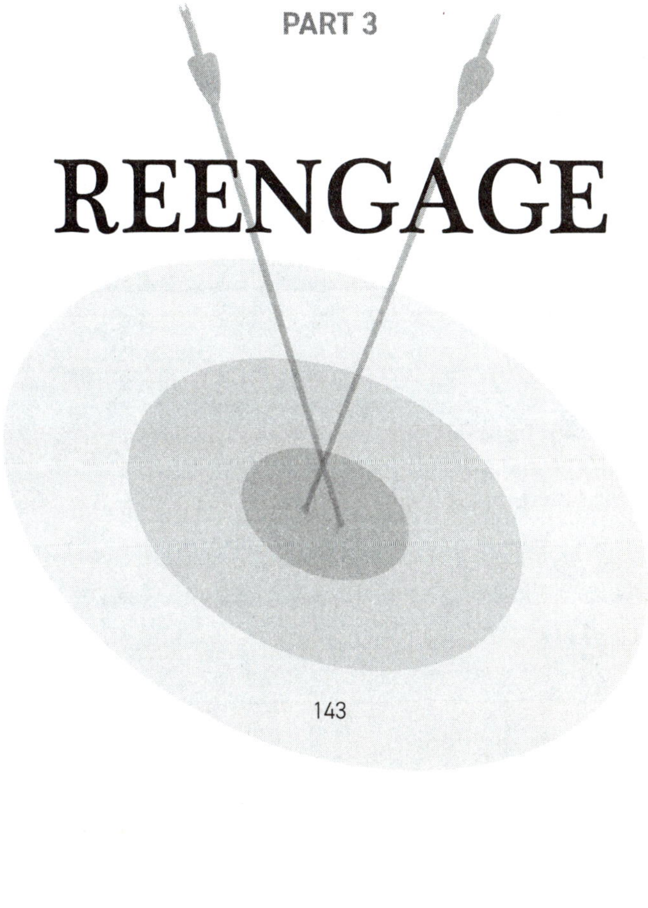

CHAPTER 7

THE SUCCESS QUESTION: HOW DO YOU DEFINE THE WIN?

I've learned that people will forget what you said, people will forget what you did, but people will never forget how made them feel.

—Maya Angelou

I know plenty of people who have lots of money, massive homes, expensive cars, and take incredible vacations, but they're miserable because their relationships are a train wreck. Years ago, seminary professor Howard Hendricks quoted someone who said, "All my life, I've been climbing the ladder of success, but I just realized it was leaning against the wrong wall."

Decades ago, the *Chicago Tribune* published part of an Ann Landers column for Father's Day. It reflected the perspective of a son toward his father at different stages of the son's life:

4 Years: My daddy can do anything.

7 Years: My dad knows a lot, a whole lot.

8 Years: My father doesn`t know quite everything.

12 Years: Oh, well, naturally Father doesn`t know that, either.

14 Years: Father? Hopelessly old-fashioned.

21 Years: Oh, that man is out-of-date. What did you expect?

25 Years: He knows a little bit about it, but not much.

30 Years: Maybe we ought to find out what Dad thinks.

35 Years: A little patience. Let`s get Dad`s assessment before we do anything.

50 Years: I wonder what Dad would have thought about that. He was pretty smart.

60 Years: My dad knew absolutely everything!

65 Years: I`d give anything if Dad were here, so I could talk this over with him. I really miss that man.[39]

Throughout my life, I've known wealthy people and poor people, the famous and the unknown, those who have immense power and those who are powerless, some who are brilliant and many who have average intelligence. But I can tell you that the only ones who are truly happy and content are those who have rich, deep, meaningful relationships, primarily with their families. Most people draw the line between success and failure by wealth, influence, power, and intelligence, but true success is measured by the love we give and receive in our cherished relationships.

39 "Child's-Eye View of Dad, Through the Ages," Anne Landers, *Chicago Tribune*, 21 June 1987, https://www.chicagotribune.com/news/ct-xpm-1987-06-21-8702160491-story.html.

At every point in our lives, we want to be able to say, "Those who know me best love and respect me the most." Let's look at success at home and at work—the double win.

At every point in our lives, we want to be able to say, "Those who know me best love and respect me the most."

INVEST IN YOUR MARRIAGE

Even if you're not married but you desire to find a mate or remarry someday, these principles are vitally important. And if you're married, there are thousands of books, podcasts, and seminars on how to have a great marriage and raise wonderful children. (I should know; I've written a few of them!) But it doesn't have to be that complicated. As the Scriptures remind us, "Love covers a multitude of sins" (1 Peter 4:8, ESV).

Back in the Dark Ages when smart TV technology was new, Michelle and I had an evening to ourselves. We decided to watch a movie someone had recommended on Amazon. At the time, we'd never watched a movie using streaming technology, even though we owned a Vizio Smart TV that features a lot of apps. When I sat down on the couch, I grabbed the cable remote and started channel surfing trying to find Amazon on our cable menu. After a few minutes of confusion and frustration, I asked Michelle for some help. She said she didn't have a clue. After a few more minutes of vain attempts, my frustration level was about to explode, so I picked up the user's manual and called the 1-800 number for technical support. When I explained what I was trying to do, the tech guy asked, "Are you holding the Vizio remote?"

In an exasperated tone, I said, "Yes!"

In a monotone voice, he told me, "Sir, just push the button."

I stared at the thing in my hand for a few seconds and then blurted out, "What button?"

He explained, "The button that says Amazon."

Is it possible to be equally relieved and ashamed at the same time? I asked, "Is that all I have to do?"

"Yes," he assured me. "Push the button."

When I pushed the button, I suddenly saw the Amazon icon on the screen, and within seconds, every movie imaginable was right before our very eyes.

I know what you're thinking: This guy is a complete idiot! I have to confess, you're right! I am the biggest idiot on the planet when it comes to technology. It just doesn't come easily to me. How can I take something so simple and make it so complicated? It's a gift, I guess.

When it comes to the marriage relationship, many couples do exactly the same thing. They often take something that should be simple and make it complicated. In fact, getting married is the easy part; staying married is much more challenging because you're taking two completely different individuals and putting them together under one roof. Those differences are what can make the marriage relationship beautiful . . . or they can make it complicated, frustrating, and messy.

Is it possible to simplify your marriage? I believe it is. Here are four buttons you can push to help simplify this most important relationship, and if you use them, you'll also provide the most positive environment possible for your children.

First Button: Love deeply.

What if the love we have for our spouse went beyond the transactional ("I'll give you this if you'll give me that.") to love sacrificially and unconditionally? This kind of love accepts and serves without expecting anything in return. Sadly, this kind of love is too rare in marriages, but it's possible. For us to cultivate a radically meaningful love for one another, we have to draw from the deep well of God's love for us. In his first letter, the apostle John connected the dots for us:

> *God showed how much he loved us by sending his one and only Son into the world so that we might have eternal life through him. This is real love—not that we loved God, but that he loved us and sent his Son as a sacrifice to take away our sins. Dear friends, since God loved us that much, we surely ought to love each other.* —1 John 4:9-11 (NLT)

When our hearts are filled with the love of God, His love overflows from us into the lives of those around us, especially our spouse and children. But without this life-transforming kindness, compassion, and glad sacrifice, people spend their time guarding themselves, being suspicious of each other, and manipulating to get what they want. That makes a marriage very complicated . . . and very unfulfilling.

Second Button: Forgive quickly.

Many have experienced traumatic, devastating abuse, and all of us have been hurt to some extent. Forgiveness requires honesty, wisdom, and courage. Pastor Lewis Smedes was one of the most insightful writers about forgiveness. He wrote, "When we forgive evil we do not excuse it, we do not tolerate it, we do not smother it. We look the evil full in the face, call it what it is, let its horror shock and stun and enrage us, and only then do we forgive it."[40] And he understood that hurt and anger at an offense can soon turn into soul-consuming bitterness. He warned and encouraged us:

> *Vengeance is having a videotape planted in your soul that cannot be turned off. It plays the painful scene over and over again inside your mind. . . . And each time it plays you feel the clap of pain again. . . . Forgiving turns off the videotape of pained memory. Forgiving sets you free.*[41]

If we have been hurt deeply, we will never forget those experiences, but we can choose to replace those memories with a new attitude and perspective.

If we have been hurt deeply, we will never forget those experiences, but we can choose to replace those memories with a new attitude and perspective. When we don't take the opportunity to forgive someone who hurt us, the pain doesn't go away—in spite of what people say, time doesn't heal all wounds. Instead, the wounds fester into bitterness and resentment. But again, we aren't left to our own resources. The more we experience the forgiveness Jesus has poured out on us, the more willing and able we'll be to forgive those who have offended us. The apostle Paul explained, "Get rid of all bitterness, rage, anger, harsh words, and slander, as well as all types of evil behavior. Instead, be kind to each other,

40 Lewis Smedes, *Forgive and Forget*, (New York: Harper & Row, 1984), 79-80.
41 Lewis Smedes, "Forgiveness: The Power to Change The Past," *Christianity Today*, 7 Jan. 1983.

tenderhearted, forgiving one another, just as God through Christ has forgiven you" (Ephesians 4:31-32, NIV). Do you have a hard time forgiving someone? Dive deeper into the vast ocean of God's forgiveness for you.

Third Button: Choose joy.

Most of us assume that happiness comes from pleasant circumstances: "If things are good, I'm happy! If things aren't so good, then I'm unhappy." This is a rollercoaster of emotions you don't want to ride! The truth is, there's no promise of a painless and hassle-free life. We always have some mixture of grief and gratitude, pain and joy. But we're not helpless, blown by the winds of whatever is going on at the moment. We can choose joy at any and every point, even in the most difficult times. How? By remembering that even when we're in the dark about what's going on, Jesus understands it all perfectly. Even when we see no hope for the future, Jesus promises to lead us step by step. Even when we suffer, Jesus reminds us that His suffering is the guarantee that there's light on the other side. Reality is much bigger and more wonderful than what's happening right here, right now.

In his great letter to the Romans, the apostle Paul assures us,

Yet what we suffer now is nothing compared to the glory he will reveal to us later. For all creation is waiting eagerly for that future day when God will reveal who his children really are. Against its will, all creation was subjected to God's curse. But with eager hope, the creation looks forward to the day when it will join God's children in glorious freedom from death and decay. For we know that all creation has been groaning as in the pains of childbirth right up to the present time. And we believers also groan, even though we have the Holy Spirit within us as a foretaste of future glory, for we long for our bodies to be released from sin and suffering. We, too, wait with eager hope for the day when God will give us our full rights as his adopted children, including the new bodies he has promised us. —Romans 8:18-23 (NLT)

We can choose to have joy even in the midst of difficulties, but only if we keep the perspective that incredible blessings will be ours one day, and genuine growth comes through our present struggles. Don't take yourself so seriously. Find ways to bring laughter into your marriage and in your relationship with your children. See trials as tests . . . and pass the tests!

Find ways to bring laughter into your marriage and in your relationship with your children. See trials as tests . . . and pass the tests!

Fourth Button: Live intentionally.

Marriage gets complicated when you lose your why. When we forget our why, we die slowly and painfully—emotionally, spiritually, and relationally. To simplify our marriages, we have to stay true to the vision we had in the first place. If you don't, you'll experience "vision drift" caused by all the demands, challenges, and distractions that can consume our attention. Therefore, we must live intentionally every day to make sure we're pushing the right buttons.

Love deeply, forgive quickly, choose joy, and live intentionally. That is how you make marriage (or a close friendship) simple, meaningful, and rich. These choices can become habits, and when that happens, your home will be both a haven and a launching pad for your children. Everyone will thrive. Isn't that what you really want?

INVEST IN YOUR CHILDREN

There are endless situations and circumstances that require parents to leverage their influence in their child's life. Asking the question, "What would a great father or mother do?" causes us to think through the best ways to give guidance and support to our children, no matter what stage of development they're in. Again, I want to keep things simple and clear. We'll look at three keys: direction, availability, and discipline.

First Key: Direction

The two most important days of our lives are the day we were born and the day we discovered why. As parents, one of our greatest responsibilities is to help our kids discover their why! Like us, when kids lose their why, they lose their way, and there are far too many examples of this happening—drugs, premarital sex, chronic anxiety, depression, and suicides, to name a few. One of the best ways to help kids discover their why is by helping them use their gifts (their God-given strengths), tap into their passions (their heart motivations), and face their struggles (with a strong sense of purpose). When we give direction in these areas, we put them on a road for future success to fulfill their own destiny. Our job is to raise them and release them.

The two most important days of our lives are the day we were born and the day we discovered why. As parents, one of our greatest responsibilities is to help our kids discover their why!

Second Key: Availability

One of the most valuable things we can give our children is the gift of time. Love is spelled T-I-M-E. As we've seen in other chapters, we live in a world of limitless pressures and distractions. It's easy to assume that our kids are "doing fine" while we're running on the treadmill of a busy schedule. "Being there" is, as some have said, half the battle. We may assume that it's enough to show up at their games, recitals, and field trips. That's great, but they need face-to-face, personal time with us. We need to be close enough to notice when they're happy and when they're stressed, so we can talk to them. We can be there in the critical moments of disappointment and when they're recognized for a job well done.

Availability isn't smothering a child (especially a teenager) with our presence and advice. As children grow up, they need to develop a sense of autonomy, independence, and self-confidence. These necessary traits usually come through trial and error. If we're not willing for them to fail, we'll limit their development and keep them dependent on us . . . and resentful toward us. Far too often, a parent's identity and security are tied up in a child's success. That's enormous (and unfair) pressure on the child, and it seldom has a happy ending.

Third Key: Discipline

Do you remember the Etch-A-Sketch™ toy that allowed you to draw using two little knobs? If you didn't like your artwork or you wanted to draw something different, all you had to do was shake it, and the screen became blank again. Unfortunately, too many parents are guilty of being Etch-A-Sketch™ parents. They give their kids innumerable "do overs" instead of enforcing rules and guidelines. What wasn't allowed yesterday is allowed today, which is very confusing for our kids. Wise parents love their children enough to be clear and consistent with limits.

Discipline is a grossly misunderstood word in our culture. It's not punishment, and it shouldn't be harsh. It's what athletes do to train for their sports, and it's what parents do for their kids to train them for a successful life. Let me put it this way: Discipline isn't something you do to your child but for your child. Discipline is correction driven by love.

Young people today are turned off by empty religion, but they're often drawn to the real thing. It's our role as parents to have an authentic relationship with God and model a life of faith, honesty, and courage. It's not enough to give them rigid rules and strictly enforce them. In his book, *The Grace Awakening*, pastor and author Chuck Swindoll warns us:

> *You want to mess up the minds of your children? Here's how—guaranteed! Rear them in a legalistic, tight context of external religion, where performance is more important than reality. Fake your faith. Sneak around and pretend your spirituality. Train your children to do the same. Embrace a long list of do's and don'ts publicly but hypocritically practice them privately . . . yet never own up to the fact that its hypocrisy. Act one way but live another. And you can count on it— emotional and spiritual damage will occur."*[42]

42 Charles Swindoll, *The Grace Awakening* (Nashville: Thomas Nelson, 2010), 90.

INVEST IN YOUR CAREER

Is it possible to be dedicated to a job without being obsessed with it? Certainly. That's part of the double win! It all depends on our perspective. Why are we working? How are we honoring God in our careers? It all goes back to Him.

Of the country's approximately one hundred million full-time employees, Gallup reports 51 percent are not emotionally engaged at work. In other words, they aren't motivated by their jobs. Another 16 percent are actively disengaged, meaning they gripe to their coworkers and drag office morale down. They do only the bare minimum, if that.[43] Now, more than ever, people are experiencing drudgery in their work instead of finding joy in their jobs. No wonder Monday is better known as "Moan-day." If you find yourself singing the classic country song, "Take This Job and Shove It," as you drive to work, I have good news for you. You can turn your Mondays into a mission.

Maybe you're in a situation where you don't feel your talents are fully utilized in the work you're doing. Maybe you don't enjoy the environment you work in or the people you work with. Like many, you feel overworked, underpaid, and underappreciated. It's easy to get down and discouraged. Instead of moaning and groaning about your situation, keep in mind there are people who would consider your job as a step up. It comes down to the perspective we choose toward our work.

What if you chose to approach your Monday differently? What if Monday could be meaningful, Tuesday could be terrific, and Wednesday could be wonderful? What if you could thrive on Thursday, and Friday could be fantastic? Does that sound like a bunch of unrealistic, hyped-up positive thinking? I will admit, that last line of Monday through Friday

43 Cited in *Money Watch*, 31 March 2017.

stuff was a bit cheesy, but I believe it's possible to find more purpose in your work than just seeing it as a paycheck. How?

Attitude Adjustment #1: Be thankful for the job you have.

Remember why you took the job in the first place. In the crush of responsibilities, it's easy to forget. Perhaps you find yourself doing something different than what you signed up for, or maybe you feel limited in your role. Perhaps you have more to offer than what your current role allows or your company or boss recognizes. Maybe you don't see any value in what you're doing. Focusing on the negative robs us of our joy. Except in the most toxic work environments, our attitudes can turn negatives into growth opportunities. In his book *Every Good Endeavor*, pastor and author Tim Keller says, "A job is a vocation only if someone else calls you to do it for them rather than for yourself."[44] And so our work can be a calling only if it is reimagined as a mission of service to something beyond merely our own interests. Thinking of work mainly as a means of self-fulfillment and self-realization slowly crushes a person.

Attitude Adjustment #2: Be faithful right now.

You may not be where you want to be right now or where you will be in the future, but you can choose to bloom where you're planted. Use your now to get you to your next. Keep giving your best. Approach your Mondays with new meaning and motivation. Have the attitude you want others to have. Go the extra mile. Take the initiative to make your colleagues feel appreciated. Look for the hidden opportunities in the midst of the obstacles or limitations. The late Zig Ziglar once said,

---

44 Timothy Keller, *Every Good Endeavor: Connecting Your Work to God's Work* (New York: Penguin, 2016).

"Opportunity does not lie in the job; it lies in the individual who looks at the possibilities instead of the problems."[45] Find the good in what you do each day, and infuse your environment with optimism and tenacity.

Attitude Adjustment #3: Your excellence will increase your influence.

Excellence is the pursuit of the exceptional. The word "excel" literally means to go beyond average. The quality of your work, character, trustworthiness, consistency, positive attitude, and willingness to go beyond the requirements of the job will get you noticed more than you can imagine. Many people would never see themselves stealing from their company, but it's easy to rob the company by spending time checking Facebook or scrolling through Instagram when no one is looking, or spending too much time shooting the breeze with coworkers on company time. Commit yourself to being a person of excellence because your commitment will increase your influence with those you work for and work with.

When you change your perspective of why you work and how you work, it changes the way you work. You can turn your mundane into a mission. Perhaps your mission is to brighten someone else's day, lend a helping hand to someone who feels overwhelmed, or give a word of encouragement to someone who doesn't feel appreciated. To quote Zig Ziglar again, "You can have everything in life you want if you will just help enough other people get what they want."[46]

---

45 Zig Ziglar, *Over the Top* (Nashville: Thomas Nelson, 1997), 88.
46 Zig Ziglar and John P. Hayes, *Network Marketing for Dummies* (Foster City, CA: IDG Books, 2006), chapter 23.

When you change your perspective of why you work and how you work, it changes the way you work.

DON'T PUT IT OFF

Marriage. Children. Career. Well, I guess we've solved them all in this chapter! No, we've just begun. In fact, many of us find all kinds of excuses to avoid making necessary changes. We put them off, but time is a precious and fleeting commodity.

The psalmist prays,

> *Lord, remind me how brief my time on earth will be. Remind me that my days are numbered—how fleeting my life is. You have made my life no longer than the width of my hand. My entire lifetime is just a moment to you; at best, each of us is but a breath.* —Psalm 39:4-5 (NLT)

How can we take advantage of the time God has given us? How can we use that time to make a difference in these three most important areas of our lives? Let me offer an effective strategy:

1) Be honest about your less-than-stellar habits.

   Do you procrastinate? Are you grouchy? Do you come home from work and veg out instead of interacting with your family? Do you eat too much, watch too much television, spend too much time on social media, complain about your boss every chance you get, or any of a hundred other bad habits? Look in the mirror long enough to see the truth about them. And if you can't see them, ask your spouse, your older children, your best friend, or a trusted colleague to be brutally honest with you. Write them down. Honestly . . . change starts here.

2) Identify the payoffs.

   Every bad habit has a payoff, or at least a perceived one. What do you gain from putting off assignments, eating a second helping, numbing your mind in front of the television or playing video games, and griping about anyone and everything? Can't figure it out? Let me help you. Every counterproductive behavior gives us something we want—and we want it more than we want change: a surge of endorphins, the feeling of being full, escaping the stresses we feel, or a sense of power from playing the role of a victim ("I'm better than she is. I'd never treat anyone like that!"). Write the payoff next to each bad habit.

3) Find a new payoff.

   Amazingly, we've seen the negative, painful, even self-destructive consequences of bad habits as pretty attractive! So now, we need to find results of better choices that are even more appealing. Physical health, looking better, sleeping more soundly, being appreciated for being more productive, reducing stress, and enjoying people are just a few payoffs for better choices. Next to each bad habit, describe a new habit and the payoff you expect from each one.

4) Don't quit.

   How many times have people made resolutions to change but then bailed out after a week or two? Change seldom happens quickly. The questions we need to ask are: Is tenacity worth the price? Will I keep going in the not-encouraging-time between the initial enthusiasm and the genuine fulfillment? The middle period is when most people quit, so build in some benchmarks of progress, and find someone to encourage you. If you don't have these identifiable marks of progress, you'll wonder if you're making any progress at all. And if you don't have someone to be your cheerleader, you may get too discouraged.

The topics in this chapter are the most important. If you succeed in them, you'll have a meaningful, love-filled life. If you fail in these, all the money, possessions, titles, and beauty in the world can't fill the gaping hole.

THE SUCCESS QUESTION:

How do you define the win?

→| Key principle: Those who know you best love you the most. |←

THINK ABOUT IT:

1) Which of the points about investing in your marriage—love deeply, forgive quickly, choose joy, and live intentionally—do you need to apply today? What difference will it make?
2) Which of the points about investing in your children—giving direction, being available, and providing loving discipline—need some attention? What are some specific adjustments you'll make?
3) Which of the attitude adjustments—be thankful for your job, be faithful right now, and commit to excellence—do you need to work on? Who will notice?

4) Why do you think it's important to identify the payoffs of bad habits and then identify better ones to encourage change?
5) Take some time to reflect and write your analysis of why bad habits have looked attractive to you, what better habits and payoffs will be, and what you need to keep you going on this new path. You can use this template for each habit:
   - Bad habit:
   - The attractive but unhelpful payoff:
   - A better habit:
   - A more attractive payoff:
   - Sources of strength and tenacity:
6) Do you think a "double win" at home and at work is really possible for you? Explain your answer.

CHAPTER 8

THE LEGACY QUESTION: HOW WILL YOU INFLUENCE THE NEXT GENERATION?

Carve your name on hearts, not tombstones. A legacy is etched into the minds of others and the stories they share about you.

—Shannon Alder

In November of 2019, our family took the trip of a lifetime. We called it "The Legacy Trip." Michelle's parents, Rod and Linda Masteller, planned meticulously and saved, so they could take our family of twenty to Israel. Even though Rod and Linda had been to Israel over a dozen times, they said this trip was the most meaningful because it was a ten-day private tour designed just for our immediate family. My in-laws wanted to do something for their four daughters, their sons-in-law, and their eleven grandkids that would mark their lives forever.

Rod and Linda knew how life-changing it had been for them to travel to Israel—to walk where Jesus walked gives you a perspective that's hard to put into words. Before we went, I had heard people say their trip to Israel made the Bible come to life. Now that I've been there, I agree—there's no experience like it. We had our own guide who designed our trip to the birthplace of Jesus in Bethlehem, His childhood home in Nazareth, the Sea of Galilee where Jesus walked on water, and the shores where He performed so many of His miracles, like feeding the five thousand.

The ultimate highlights of the trip were having a family prayer gathering in the Garden of Gethsemane, seeing the place where Jesus was crucified, and ending our tour at the garden tomb where Jesus had been buried and where He had risen from the dead. Throughout the trip, my father-in-law taught from the Bible and shared what each site meant to him. He explained the importance of living according the truths of the Bible and fulfilling God's purposes.

At the time, my father-in-law had been a pastor for over fifty years and had dedicated his life to fulfill his calling to serve God in full-time ministry. He used to say that the three most important things in life are your relationship with the Lord, your family, and your health. Nothing else was more important to him than those three things. His definition of success was "Those who know you best love you the most." Rod and Linda enjoyed fifty-three years of marriage. They have four beautiful, godly daughters, and eleven grandchildren. Little did we know that about a year after we took "The Legacy Trip" to Israel, God would call Rod home to heaven at the age of seventy-five.

My father-in-law was one of the hundreds of thousands of people who lost their lives to COVID-19. It was a complete shock and an unexpected page of our family's story. But now we understand why this trip was so important to him. It was as if he knew his final days were drawing near. Looking back, we see how God orchestrated the timing of events that would allow Rod to fulfill his dream of taking his kids and grandkids on a trip that would mark their lives forever and serve as the legacy he wanted to leave us. One of our most treasured photographs is a group picture on the Mount of Olives overlooking the city of Jerusalem. We wore our "Legacy 3:10" T-shirts. The "3:10" comes from Rod's life verse, Philippians 3:10: "I want to know Christ and experience the mighty power that raised him from the dead. I want to suffer with him, sharing in his death."

Rod knew that leaving a lasting legacy isn't about material possessions or just fun memories, but ultimately, leaving a foundation of faith that would impact generations.

Like Michelle, I've been blessed by being raised in a Christian home and having godly parents to serve as examples of God's love and God's ways. I'm the youngest of four sons, and I'm grateful for the rich heritage of faith that my mother and father taught me and my brothers, and later, their grandchildren. Michelle and I have three grown children and two sons-in-law, and we're very grateful for their relationships with God and their commitment to serve Him at home and at work.

REDEFINITION

When you hear the word "inheritance," what comes to mind? House, land, jewelry, collections of ornaments, furniture, investment accounts? Sure, that's what we normally think about when someone uses that word, but I suggest we put on a different set of lenses and look again. The most important inheritance we leave our children and grandchildren isn't what we leave for them but what we leave in them—the intangible but priceless gifts of good values, an example worth following, a faith that stands up to tests, and memories of joy and courage.

The most important inheritance we leave our children and grandchildren isn't what we leave for them but what we leave in them.

Psalm 78 is a chronicle of the history of Israel. As part of the introduction, the writer explains the importance of this story:

> *We've heard true stories from our fathers about our rich heritage. We will continue to tell our children and not hide from the rising generation the great marvels of our God—his miracles and power that have brought us all this far. The story of Israel is a lesson in God's ways. He established decrees for Jacob and established the law in Israel, and he commanded our forefathers to teach them to their children. For perpetuity, God's ways will be passed down from one generation to the next, even to those not yet born. In this way, every generation will have a living faith in the laws of life and will never forget the faithful ways of God.* —Psalm 78:3-7

Today, a lot of people have invested in genealogical studies to trace their ancestors back as far as possible. Sometimes, it confirms what our grandparents told us about the family's history, but occasionally, we get a shock. For example, one person learned she is the 26x great-granddaughter of King Edward III of England and the royal line before him. On the other end of the spectrum, another woman discovered she's the 9x great-granddaughter of someone who was hanged as a witch in Salem in 1692.[47]

You may not be descended from a king or a witch (you never know!), but someday, future generations will look back and see what kind of impact you left on your family. Can one person really make a difference? Absolutely! Parallel studies where made of two men, Jonathan Edwards and Max Jukes, who lived in America about the same time in the 1700s. Edwards was one of the foremost theologians and philosophers in American history. His heirs include:

> *1 U.S. Vice-President, 1 Dean of a law school, 1 dean of a medical school, 3 U.S. Senators, 3 governors, 3 mayors, 13 college presidents, 30 judges, 60 doctors, 65 professors, 75 military officers, 80 public office holders, 100 lawyers, 100 clergymen, and 285 college graduates.*[48]

When a sociologist discovered that 42 men in New York prisons were descendants of Max Jukes, he dug deeper into the family's story and found that his progeny included:

> *7 murderers, 60 thieves, 190 prostitutes, 150 other convicts, 310 paupers, and 440 who were physically wrecked by addiction to alcohol. Of the 1,200 descendants that were studied, 300 died prematurely.*[49]

We may assume that our influence is limited to one generation, but that's not the case. Our lives have a profound impact on people decades and even centuries after we've died.

---

47 "3 Crazy Things Real People Have Found in Their Family Trees," *Ancestry*, 10 Nov. 2015, https://blogs.ancestry.com/cm/3-crazy-things-real-people-have-found-in-their-family-trees/.
48 Larry Ballard "Family Ministries," *YWAM*, 1 July 2017, https://www.ywam-fmi.org/news/multigenerational-legacies-the-story-of-jonathan-edwards/.
49 Larry Ballard, "Family Ministries". . . .

PRINTING AND IMPRINTING

In recent years, printing technology has gone to a new level of sophistication. Some time ago, Michelle was walking through the airport in Dallas, and she saw an exhibit of famous women whose images had been reproduced in three-dimensional models. The copies didn't have the fine qualities of each strand of hair and gradients of skin color; instead, they were orange. They demonstrated the newest technology, but I'm sure the day is coming when we won't be able to tell the copy from the real thing!

If imitation is the sincerest form of flattery, imprinting is the most powerful force to shape young lives. In our book, *Family Shift*, Michelle and I shared the story from a National Geographic program that described the work of biologists who were raising whooping crane chicks from eggs. To acclimate the young birds to what would become their real world, the scientists dressed up in white baggy suits with one arm extended as the neck and the hand painted to look like an adult crane's head. It was a comical sight, but this effort was amazingly effective. Young birds—and young humans—mimic what they see, hear, and feel in their relationships with scientist-cranes or moms and dads (and aunts, uncles, and grandparents).

Family members have the greatest impact on young lives, but coaches, teachers, bosses, and neighbors can also make a positive impression. One of the most powerful relationships described in the Bible was between the prophet Elijah and his protégé Elisha. After the younger man had been with the prophet for a long time and had seen God's hand on him, Elijah prepared him for his departure. The historian takes us to the scene:

> *When they reached the other side, Elijah said to Elisha, "What can I do for you before I'm taken from you? Ask anything." Elisha said, "our life repeated in my life. I want to be a holy man just like you."* —2 Kings 2:9 (MSG)

"Your life repeated in my life. I want to be just like you." —2 Kings 2:9 (MSG)

"Your life repeated in my life. I want to be just like you." That line hit me like a ton of bricks. Our children may not express it in exactly the same way, but that's their built-in desire . . . unless something disrupts the relationship and disappoints them. A song that poignantly describes this disruption is Harry Chapin's "Cat's in the Cradle." A father is too preoccupied with his work to spend time with his son, who still idolized his father: "I'm gonna be like you, Dad. You know I'm gonna be like you." The verses go through the child growing up and the father's continued distraction with work. The son pleads with his father to throw a ball with him, but the dad excused himself, "Not today. I got a lot to do." At the end of the song, the boy has grown into a man with a family of his own. The now older father narrates:

I've long since retired; my son's moved away. I called him up just the other day. I said, "I'd like to see you if you don't mind." He said, "I'd love to Dad, if I could find the time." You see my new job's a hassle, and the kids have the flu. But it's sure nice talking to you, Dad, It's been sure nice talking to you. . . ." And as I hung up the phone it had occurred to me He'd grown up just like me. My boy was just like me.[50]

The lyrics are haunting . . . and challenging . . . and inspiring. What can we do to shape (or change) our legacy?

50 "Cat's in the Cradle," Sung by Harry Chapin, written by Harry Chapin, Warner Chappell Music, Inc., 1974.

A 3D LEGACY

When my father-in-law passed away, Michelle, along with our entire family, experienced a time of grief and reflection. The mark Rod left on us continues to this day and will endure in our children and grandchildren as part of his amazing legacy. Actually, working through the pain of grief has produced tremendous growth in our lives.

Michelle dove into reading her father's Bible and the handwritten notes from his daily devotions. Gradually, she began to understand the importance of leaving a permanent mark on those around us, especially our children. She developed a message she delivered on Mother's Day following her dad's passing and shared it with our church. It was titled, "3Ds to Live Your Legacy." It was powerful, and it inspired many people that day. She shared three concrete, specific steps we can take to build our legacy for future generations. I've adopted these principles too:

Decide what your legacy will be.

But doesn't it just happen? Yes, if we don't have a vision and a plan for it, we'll leave a legacy, but maybe not the one that inspires our kids and grandkids. The first decision is to shift our mentality away from leaving things to leaving themes, not valuables but values. As Stephen Covey famously put it: "Begin with the end in mind." No one plans to leave the kind of emptiness and heartache described in Chapin's song, but if we're as preoccupied as that father, that's the predictable result. Making excuses doesn't cut it. We have to do better than that.

The first decision is to shift our mentality away from leaving things to leaving themes, not valuables but values.

Examine your past. What is the legacy your parents and grandparents left you? Is it rich and meaningful, or do you need to change the script, so you leave a different legacy? A friend of mine told me one of his grandfathers was the meanest man he'd ever known, and his father had been emotionally crippled in that toxic home. My friend decided that he would do better—he had to do better—in his relationship with his children.

Examine your present. What's the state of your relationships with your kids today? What values are they absorbing in the atmosphere of your home? Do they pick up kindness, wisdom, and strength from you? What do they hear you praise? How do they see you treat your spouse, your friends, your colleagues at work? What do they hear you gripe about? Do they know you delight in them?

Examine your future. No matter how poorly you've communicated, how many mistakes you've made, or what hurt you've suffered and caused, God will give you the power to change the direction of your life and your legacy. You may feel stuck, but you're not. You may have let bitterness cloud every relationship, but you can receive and extend forgiveness. You may have been a terrible example, but you can repent and change the story. It may not be easy, but all things are possible through the grace and power of God.

Determine how you'll make your mark.

My father-in-law used to say, "Life isn't a chance; it's a choice." He also reminded me, "Life isn't made up of what you do in a day, but what you do daily." Intentions will only take you so far. You have to create habits that shape your ability to make positive marks on the people you love.

» The mark of your convictions

What is the source of your most deeply held beliefs? Your parents' words when you were a child? The anger of political pundits? The internal nudges toward tempting vices? Or the Word of God? A recent survey found that 65 percent of Americans identified themselves as Christians, but only 11 percent read the Bible daily.[51] When you read the Bible, are you bored and just want to check it off as a discipline, or does it challenge you, amaze you, and thrill you? We can get in the Word, but that's not enough; we need the Word to get into us!

I've always found a particular passage to be more than a gentle nudge to lean into God. The writer to the Hebrews tells us,

For the word of God is alive and powerful. It is sharper than the sharpest two-edged sword, cutting between soul and spirit, between joint and marrow. It exposes our innermost thoughts and desires. Nothing in all creation is hidden from God. Everything is naked and exposed before his eyes, and he is the one to whom we are accountable. —Hebrews 4:12-13 (NLT)

» The mark of your character

We spend an incredible amount of time and money in search of an easy life, and for the most part, we've found it! Our grandparents

51 "Measuring Religion in Pew Research Center's American Trends Panel," *Pew Research Center's Religion & Public Life Project*, 14 Jan. 2021, https://www.pewforum.org/2021/01/14/measuring-religion-in-pew-research-centers-american-trends-panel/.

would be (or are) amazed that we have it so good. This pursuit may be normal and natural, but it's soul-numbing. Character is shaped in times of testing. Like an athlete working out with weights, the reps make him feel weaker, but he's actually getting stronger. My father-in-law wisely observed, "Tough times don't make or break you. They reveal you."

The apostle James began his letter with a challenge and a promise:

Dear brothers and sisters, when troubles of any kind come your way, consider it an opportunity for great joy. For you know that when your faith is tested, your endurance has a chance to grow. So let it grow, for when your endurance is fully developed, you will be perfect and complete, needing nothing. —James 1:2-4 (NLT)

We may not like this message, and we may want to blot passages like this out of our Bibles, but we need this truth more than ever.

Problems, pressure, and people shape our character. We don't have to manufacture tests. If we follow Jesus, we'll certainly experience our fair share. If, though, we're seldom uncomfortable, it's a pretty good sign that we're following someone besides Jesus!

Do people see the sweetness, humility, kindness, and inner strength of Jesus in you? Are these qualities growing in the fertile soil of faith, or are they wasting away in the boiling cauldron of our loud and angry times?

» The mark of your communication

One of the most powerful legacies we can leave our children is for them to hear us pray for them—often. Yes, I know, some people feel very uncomfortable praying out loud, but it's just expressing your heart to someone who loves you. Are you afraid of making a mistake, of saying something wrong? Welcome to the club! We're finite, and He's infinite. We're going to get it wrong sometimes. Practice may not make perfect prayers, but it's a wonderful way to reinforce what's important in our relationships with our children.

Another legacy we leave our children is the pattern of affirming, healing words. Our speech is a reflection of what's in our hearts, and it has the power to do great good or great harm. The apostle Paul instructed the Ephesians:

> *Don't use foul or abusive language. Let everything you say be good and helpful, so that your words will be an encouragement to those who hear them. And do not bring sorrow to God's Holy Spirit by the way you live. Remember, he has identified you as his own, guaranteeing that you will be saved on the day of redemption.* —Ephesians 4:29-30

When was the last time you did an accounting of what comes out of your mouth? It's a sobering exercise and a necessary one.

» The mark of your confidence

Many people have a shallow view of humility. They assume that it means we shy away from any conflict, let people have their way all the time, and keep our mouths shut. That's humiliation, not humility! Moses was known as the most humble man who ever lived, and he was as bold as a lion. Humility is seeing yourself through God's eyes: a masterpiece, yet flawed; deeply loved, but capable of self-pity and self-righteousness. Perhaps, ironically, seeing ourselves more clearly takes the blinders off and lets us be more honest with God, more understanding of others, and freed up to be bold when it's appropriate. God knows the worst about us . . . and loves us still. The writer to the Hebrews instructed,

So do not throw away your confidence; it will be richly rewarded. You need to persevere so that when you have done the will of God, you will receive what he has promised." —Hebrews 10:35-36 (NIV)

Dare to be intentional.

If we want to leave a legacy, we need to take steps in the right direction—and we need to start today! We aren't promised tomorrow. Life is fleeting, so make the most of every day.

» Be intentional because time is short.

Moses prayed, "So teach us to number our days, that we may gain a heart of wisdom" (Psalm 90:12, NKJV). The great British preacher Charles H. Spurgeon commented, "Men who are led by the reflection upon the brevity of time give their earnest attention to eternal things."[52] Treasure today. Make it meaningful.

» Be intentional in creating memories.

At the end of Genesis, Jacob was an old man who was about to die. He called his sons to come near and blessed each one, and he said, "May my name be an echo in their lives" (Genesis 48:16, MSG). In other words, he wanted them to remember his love, his integrity, and his honor every time they heard or said his name. That's how those qualities would be reinforced, and that's how they'd be repeated in his sons' lives and for generations to come.

Most of us have at least some pleasant memories of our childhoods and the love we shared with people in our families. Take some time to scan your mind to locate these memories. What happened? Why was it meaningful? What are you doing to create great

52 C. H. Spurgeon, *The Treasury of David* . . . 2nd ed., vol. 4 (New York: Funk & Wagnalls, 1883) 203.

memories for your children and grandchildren? What can you do better?

» Be intentional with your actions.

All the good ideas and plans don't amount to much . . . unless they're put into action. I suggest you look at the values, character, and love you can impart daily, monthly, and yearly. For instance:

Reevaluate your schedule so you can spend time with your children at breakfast and dinner. I know you're busy. I know they're busy. But make this time a priority, so you can connect with them every day. Yes, every day.

Once a week, take your spouse on a date, and once a week, do something fun as a family. Game nights, a hike, riding bicycles, volunteer together, or any of hundreds of other things that will give you opportunities to laugh together and share experiences.

At least once a year, take a trip together. You can go camping, or you can go to a five-star resort. I don't think it matters what you do or how much or how little money you spend, just so you spend time enjoying each other.

THE SHORT AND LONG OF IT

When Michelle speaks on the importance of building a legacy, she explains, "Life is short, so be intentional. Life is long, so stay encouraged."

Life is short, so be intentional. Life is long, so stay encouraged.

Jesus is the author and the finisher of our faith. He is the Alpha and the Omega, the beginning and the end. What He starts, He finishes. He can see us through to victory. He makes beauty from ashes. He turns graves into gardens. He can cause beautiful things to come out of the most broken and scarred places in our lives, but He gives us the dignity of choice. Will we invite Him in and give Him the keys to our hearts and our homes?

My prayer is: "Lord, give me a multigenerational vision for my life." Make it your prayer, too. Whether you're a parent, a grandparent, or a great-grandparent, or maybe an aunt, an uncle, a teacher, or a coach, you have a powerful influence over young lives. God has given you an important role to play. His call on us is to fight for the hearts and minds of our children for four generations. Until God calls us home, we have a battle to fight for the hearts and minds of our children. Fight well.

THE LEGACY QUESTION:

How will you influence the next generation?

→| Key Principle: What you leave in them is more important than what you leave for them. |←

THINK ABOUT IT:

1) What is the legacy of values and character your parents and grandparents have passed down to you? How do you think that legacy has affected you and your most important relationships?

2) Why do we (or many of us, at least) avoid tests of character and patience? What do we miss when we avoid them? What is the payoff for facing them?
3) Imagine what you'd like people to say at your funeral and write out the key statements.
4) How can you adjust your schedule to spend quality time with your spouse and children daily, weekly, and yearly? Focus on daily and weekly.
5) What changes will make the most difference?
6) Do you expect your own internal resistance or pushback from the people in your family? If you do, how will you handle it?
7) What is the most important takeaway you've gotten from reading this book and reflecting on the principles?

ABOUT THE AUTHOR

Rodney Gage is the founding and lead pastor of ReThink Life Church and is the president of Engage The Family, a ministry committed to helping families build strong relationships. Over the span of thirty years of ministry, he has spoken to thousands of people worldwide through special events, church services, and conferences. Rodney has also spoken to over two million students in public and private schools and has appeared on over 150 television, radio, and podcasts interviews. He is the author of seven books, including his latest two books, *ReThink Life*, and *Family Shift*, cowritten with his wife, Michelle. The Gages have three adult children and live in Orlando, Florida. Rodney is a graduate of Liberty University and Southwestern Seminary.

COURSES
By Rodney & Michelle Gage

Family Shift

- 6 part video teaching features Rodney & Michelle Gage's S.H.I.F.T. Method for building strong family relationships.
- The course also includes a digital companion workbook perfect for individual and small group discussions.

The Double Win

The ideal resource to use for a small group or Lunch and Learn for your church or business.

- 9 part video teaching on the Double Win principles by Rodney Gage
- The course also includes a digital companion workbook.

The Winning Family Podcast

The Winning Family Podcast with Rodney & Michelle Gage is designed to help you win at home and in life. Each episode features hope, and how-to's and answers the tough questions couples and parents ask to help you win in your most important relationships.

Schedule Rodney Gage to Speak At Your Church or Corporate Event.

ONE DAY or ONE NIGHT EVENTS: HELP YOUR CHURCH EXPERIENCE THE DOUBLE WIN

Schedule Rodney Gage to speak at your church for a one-night event or during your Sunday morning worship experiences as he shares his powerful message on The Winning Family. During this one-night event, couples, parents, and business leaders will experience a 90-minute workshop where Rodney Gage shares his 8-step framework designed to help parents win at home & work. Through learning and laughter, attendees will receive hope, help, and how-to's to experience the Double Win in their own lives.

HELP YOUR BUSINESS EXPERIENCE THE DOUBLE WIN

Schedule Rodney Gage to lead his Double Win workshop for your company. During this one-day workshop, employees will learn winning strategies to help them win at home and work. Through learning, laughter, and personal interaction with Rodney Gage, employees will discover the ultimate win-win so they can thrive.

To schedule Rodney Gage go to thewinningfamily.com